SS-Totenkopf

SS-TOTENKOPF

THE HISTORY OF THE 'DEATH'S HEAD' DIVISION 1940–45

Dr. Chris Mann

MBI Publishing Company

This edition first published in 2001 by
MBI Publishing Company
729 Prospect Avenue
PO Box 1, Osceola
WI 54020-0001 USA

MBI Publishing Company books are also available at discounts in bulk quantity
for industrial or sales-promotional use. For details write to Special Sales Manager
at Motorbooks International Wholesalers & Distributors, 729 Prospect Avenue,
PO Box 1, Osceola, WI 54020-0001 USA.

Library of Congress Cataloging-in-Publication Data available.

ISBN: 0-7603-1015-7

Editorial and design by
Amber Books Ltd
Bradley's Close
74-77 White Lion Street
London
N1 9PF

Project Editor: Charles Catton
Editor: Siobhan O'Connor
Design: Roger Hyde
Picture Research: Lisa Wren

Printed and bound in Italy by: Eurolitho S.p.A., Cesano Boscone (MI)

PICTURE CREDITS

AKG London: 16, 36-37, 38, 66, 69, 142. **Robert Hunt Library**: 58-59. **Suddeutscher Verlag**: 6, 12, 14, 20-21
(both), 23, 24, 25, 28-29, 30-31, 84, 108, 143, 151, 156, 158, 164. **TRH Pictures**: 8, 9, 10, 15, 19, 27, 32, 33, 34, 39,
40, 42, 43, 44-45, 46, 47, 48, 50-51, 55, 56, 57 (IWM), 60, 61, 62, 64-65, 70, 72-73, 75, 76, 78, 80, 81, 82, 86, 87, 88,
90, 92, 94, 95, 96, 98 (US National Archives), 99, 100-101, 102, 103, 105, 107, 110, 112, 113, 114-115, 116-117
(both), 118-119, 120, 121, 122, 124-125, 127, 128, 130, 131, 132-133, 134, 135, 136, 138, 140, 144, 146, 148, 149,
150, 152-153, 154, 159, 160, 162, 167, 169, 170, 172-173, 175 (Bundesarchivs), 176, 179, 181, 182 (IWM), 183,
184, 186.

Map artworks by Hardlines

Contents

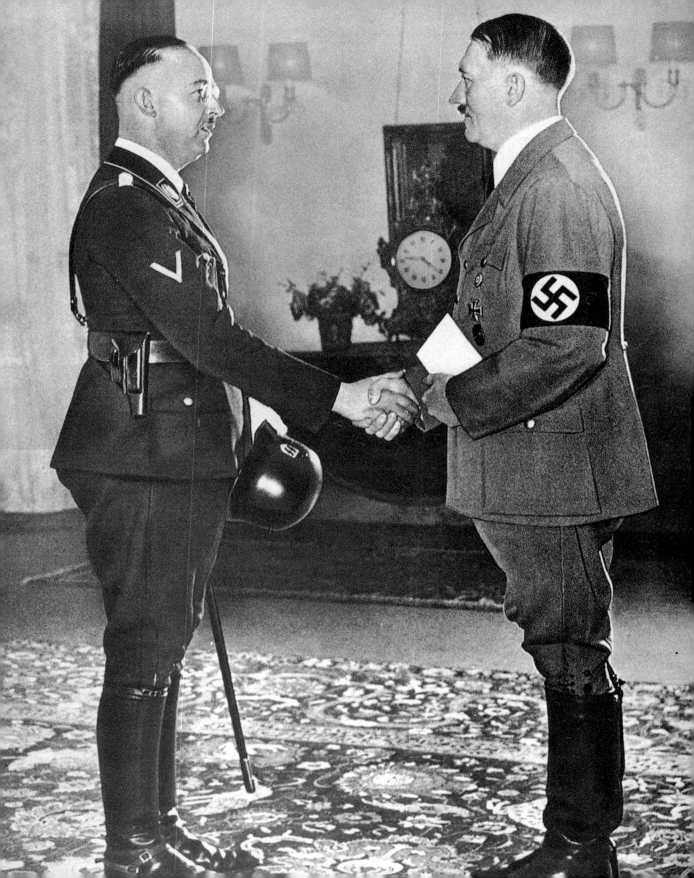

CHAPTER ONE

FOUNDATION

The *Totenkopf* Division inspired awe in every unit that faced it. The product largely of one man's vision, the division epitomised the best and worst aspects of the *Waffen-SS*, capable of extreme bravery and courage, but also some of the worst atrocities of the war.

The *Waffen-SS* earned a fearsome combat reputation in World War II. By May 1945, more than 800,000 men had served in its 38 divisions and some 20–25 per cent of them had been killed in battle. *Waffen-SS* formations fought on all fronts except the Western Desert and, in particular, played a critical role on the Eastern Front in the war against the Soviet Union. Yet despite the *Waffen-SS*'s high standing within the German armed forces, the *Wehrmacht*, this reputation largely rested on a half dozen or so first-class fighting formations. The 3rd SS Panzer Division *Totenkopf* was part of this inner core of elite SS formations. The *Totenkopf*, or Death's Head, Division saw service in France in 1940. It also took part in Operation Barbarossa, the invasion of the Soviet Union in 1941, and thereafter was involved in some of the bitterest fighting on the Eastern Front: at Demyansk, at Kursk, outside Warsaw and, towards the end of the war, around Budapest. The division fought with bravery and tenacity throughout the conflict, and Hitler and many senior Wehrmacht commanders, such as Erich von Manstein, considered the

Left: The *Reichsführer-SS* and his Führer shake hands. Heinrich Himmler's SS empire contained the concentration camp system and the *Waffen-SS*, the two key institutions in *Totenkopf*'s history.

Totenkopf Division one of Nazi Germany's best and most reliable fighting formations.

Totenkopf's ferocity and ability to endure in battle were legendary. The men of the division were manifestly not *Soldaten wie die anderen auch* ('just soldiers like the others'), as postwar German chancellor Konrad Adenauer is reputed to have described the members of the *Waffen-SS* in 1953. The division's background, the personality of its founder Theodor Eicke and the traditions, motivation and ideology of the *Waffen-SS* meant that *Totenkopf* was not just another military formation. As Robert Koehl noted in his book *The Black Corps*: 'Tradition, that familiar concept in military annals, had its influence in the SS too, and not always as desired by SS commanders – or by SS volunteers – forcing the man to become both more than himself, and a good deal less.'

The unit's formidable combat reputation rested on a ruthless and brutal criminality when it came to the treatment of enemy prisoners-of-war or civilians. It is worth noting that five of the most well-known and well-documented atrocities committed by the *Waffen-SS* – the massacres of Le Paradis, Tulle, Oradour-sur-Glane, Malmedy and the reprisal killings on the Arno – were either carried out by *Totenkopf* units or were associated with men who were products of the *Totenkopf* Division. This is quite apart from the

division's intimate involvement in the SS-run concentration camp system.

The *Waffen-SS* produced men such as Fritz Knöchlein, Heinz Lammerding, Hermann Preiss and Max Simon. Fritz Knöchlein commanded the 14th Company of *Totenkopf*'s 2nd Battalion at Le Paradis; Heinz Lammerding was the ex-operations officer of the *Totenkopf* Division who, as commander of the 2nd SS Division *Das Reich*, ordered the massacres of French civilians at Tulle and Oradour; Hermann Preiss, *SS-Gruppenführer* (Major General) and briefly divisional commander of *Totenkopf*, was prosecuted for the massacre of US troops at Malmedy, Belgium, by troops of his then command, 1st SS Panzer Division *Leibstandarte* Adolf Hitler; and Max Simon, long-term stalwart of the Death's Head Division, ordered the reprisal killings at Arno. To understand the environment which created such men, it is worth examining the origins of the Nazi Party, the SS, the *Waffen-SS* and the concentration camp system.

THE ORIGINS OF THE SS

As a soldier in the Bavarian Reserve Infantry Regiment 16 in World War I, Adolf Hitler found a

Left: Adolf Hitler (on right of picture) with two comrades from World War I, Ernst Schmidt and Max Amann. Hitler found a sense of purpose in his military service, and was embittered by Germany's defeat.

sense of comradeship, discipline and a cause for the first time in his life. On 11 November 1918, the war ended while Hitler was convalescing in hospital in Pomerania, after being gassed in Belgium. He was horrified by the news of defeat and recalled from his hospital bed that he now 'knew everything was lost. Only fools – liars or criminals – could hope for mercy from the enemy. In these nights my hatred grew against the men who had brought about this crime.'

The return to civilian life was impossibly difficult for numerous veterans of World War I. Many were surprised by the suddenness of Germany's collapse and, like Hitler, felt that their country's civilian leadership had betrayed them. They also returned home to political chaos, hunger and revolution, as extremist groups tried to seize power. Plenty of ex-German soldiers had no desire to return to disdain, unemployment and even possible starvation. These men proved ready recruits for the *Freikorps*, the paramilitary force used by the embattled new German Government to suppress the attempted communist takeover of early 1919 and Polish insurgents on Germany's now much-reduced eastern border. The political outlook of the *Freikorps* was largely nationalistic and right wing, and members often drifted into membership of one of the many parties that had grown up on Germany's extremist fringe.

One of those parties was the *Deutsche Arbeiter Partie* (DAP – German Workers' Party). Adolf Hitler was still on the payroll of his wartime regiment and was sent to report on the DAP's activities. He joined the party in September 1919, and such were his abilities that he rose quickly to propaganda director. Hitler subsequently had the party renamed the *Nationalsozialistische Deutsche Arbeiter Partie* (NSDAP – National Socialist German Workers' Party, usually shortened to Nazi Party from NAtional and so-ZI-alist). Hitler's rise was rapid and, by January 1922, he had manoeuvred his way into the chairmanship of the party.

Above: A product of the Prussian elite: General von Mackensen, seen here in 1940, has duelling scars visible on his cheeks. Note the death's head symbol, later adopted by *Totenkopf*, worn on his headgear.

NSDAP political meetings in the early 1920s often degenerated into running battles with left-wing groups. The NSDAP initially received protection from *Zeitfreiwilligen* (temporary volunteers) from the Munich *Reichswehr* (the Reich's Defence – German armed forces), but these men, while quite possibility sympathetic, were not the kind of devoted party supporters Hitler envisaged. Besides, their primary loyalties lay elsewhere.

Nonetheless, Ernst Röhm, a *Reichswehr* officer and local *Freikorps* leader who had liaised with Hitler in his role as informer, was impressed enough with the fledging and still minuscule party to join. Röhm, an experienced soldier and organiser of paramilitary forces, was the driving force behind the more muscular side of the NSDAP, initially known as the Sports and Gymnastic Division (SA). Röhm set about

Above: A famous shot of the *Stosstrupp Adolf Hitler* ready for action in Bayreuth, 2 September 1923. Hitler's early bodyguard were a forerunner of the SS. Ulrich Graf stands to the right of the Imperial German flag.

expanding the SA which, in November 1921, gained the new title of *Sturmabteilungen*, or storm troopers, and handily retained the same initials. The name bore connotations of the elite assault detachments of World War I, something which appealed to the hardened *Freikorps* veterans who made up most of the SA.

Hitler soon found, however, that the SA men were not entirely his to command. They were not always available to him, and owed their primary loyalty to Röhm. When Hitler attended their meetings, manoeuvres or drill parades, he was received politely, but was not allowed to control the men. In spite of this, Röhm was quite close to Hitler; he was one of the few amongst Hitler's close associates who used the familiar *du* (you) as a term of address. In March 1923,

aware of Hitler's concern, Röhm formed a Munich-based bodyguard of 12 SA men solely to protect the party leader. Hitler's new bodyguard were known as the *Stabswache* (Headquarters Guard) and they swore an oath of personal loyalty to him. Yet the *Stabswache* remained in the SA and the unit was soon disbanded after yet another quarrel with the SA leadership.

Indeed, the SA's relationship with the party remained unclear. Despite appointing Hermann Göring, a highly decorated hero of World War I and loyal comrade, to organise and command the military wing of the SA, Hitler knew that the organisation remained Röhm's private army, which refused to take orders from Nazi Party officials. Röhm's somewhat apolitical attitude was clearly stated in a memo that he sent to Hitler: 'Party politics will not be tolerated … in the SA.' Thus it was that, two months after the formation of the *Stabswache*, Hitler created a carefully selected 100-man force, the *Stosstrupp Adolf Hitler*, who were, as their name suggested, unquestionably loyal to him. The *Stosstrupp* were armed, motorised and wore military-style uniforms. By the autumn, they had reached the strength of four platoons: one infantry platoon of four squads, a machine-gun platoon, a machine-pistol platoon and a mortar platoon. They also soon adopted the death's head (skull-and-cross bones) symbol as their emblem.

The *Stosstrupp* received their badges from a stock of army surplus equipment and thereby tapped into an image with a long lineage in German military tradition. This distinctive emblem would remain a key symbol of the future SS and was divisional insignia of the 3rd SS Division *Totenkopf*. Indeed, it was the only badge shared with all SS formations – the *Allgemeine-SS* (General SS), Germanic-SS and *Waffen-SS*. Despite its sinister appearance, the death's head was chosen for its historical resonance rather than from any desire to strike fear into those who saw it. In 1741, the elite Prussian units Leib-Husaren regiments 1 and 2 adopted the symbol in honour of the Prussian king, Freidrich Wilhelm I, who had died the previous year. The German state of Brunswick also used the symbol for Hussar Regiment 17 and the 3rd Battalion of Infantry 92 during the Napoleonic Wars. The death's head emblem remained in use throughout Germany's unification and, during World War I, was chosen as a badge by a number of crack German formations such as storm troopers and tank men. It was also adopted by some of the more fearsome *Freikorps* units in the immediate postwar years. As Robin Lumsden notes in his description of SS symbolism in *SS Himmler's Black Order 1923–45*: 'Because of its association with these formations it became symbolic not only of wartime daring and self-sacrifice, but also of post war traditionalism, anti-liberalism and anti-Bolshevism.' It was an appropriate choice for the *Stosstrupp* and its successor, the SS.

The *Stosstrupp* was soon in action. Hitler, in one of the few serious misjudgments of his interwar political career, decided to take advantage of the volatile atmosphere in Bavaria in late 1923 and seize political power. The so-called 'Beer Hall' Putsch of 9 November 1923 did not, by any means, result in the Nazis sweeping to power. The police proved more than willing to open fire on Hitler and his 3000 Nazi supporters. Sixteen Nazis were killed and Hitler and most of the Nazi leadership were arrested, the NSDAP banned, and the SA and *Stosstrupp* dissolved. Although the Beer Hall Putsch had all the trappings of a fiasco, it raised Hitler from regional obscurity to national notoriety overnight. The Nazi Party also gained its first sacred relic. The banner held at the front of the column was splattered with the blood of the dying standard bearer, Andreas Bauriedl.

The so-called *Blutfahne* or blood banner was thereafter used to consecrate the standards of newly formed SS and SA units. Furthermore, the *Stosstrupp* had served its purpose, as Ulrich Graf heroically threw himself in front of a volley that might well have killed Hitler and was hit 16 times. Extraordinarily, Graf survived. Although the *Stosstrupp* was small and politically unimportant, in it Hitler saw the advantage of a loyal elite core and thus it proved to be the forerunner to the SS.

THE FORMATION OF THE SS

In December 1924, Hitler emerged from prison after serving only nine months of his five-year sentence for treason and set about rebuilding his party. The period in prison had allowed him to put on weight (the food was better than he was used to) write his manifesto *Mein Kampf* (*My Struggle*) and assess the implications of the putsch. The fiasco had convinced him that he should only employ legal methods in his quest for power when the government had the loyalty of the police and army. Hitler forbade the SA to bear arms or function as a private army. This upset Röhm, who envisaged the SA as a force which would supplement

and eventually supersede the regular *Reichswehr*, and the SA chief briefly resigned from the party.

Hitler now decided to create a dedicated bodyguard unit. In April 1925, the *Führer* (leader), as Hitler was now known, had Julius Schreck, a veteran of the *Stabswache*, re-form his bodyguard detail. Schreck initially recruited eight men, all original *Stosstrupp* veterans, who were at first called the *Schutzkommando* and then, later, the *Sturmstaffel*. However, on 9 November, the name *Schutzstaffel* (Defence Echelon or, more usually, Protection Squad) was adopted, probably at the suggestion of Hermann Göring, who had returned from exile after fleeing the government clampdown on the Nazi Party after the Beer Hall Putsch. The term was new. It was not subject to government banning orders, as so many emotive or military titles were, nor was it associated with the *Freikorps* or nationalist sports clubs. If anything, the term alluded to air warfare. This was understandable as Göring had commanded the famous Richthofen Flying Circus. The word *staffel* was widely identified with fighter aircraft on escort duties. The unit's full title – *Schutzstaffel der NSDAP* – was usually shortened to the abbreviation 'SS'.

The SS was always intended to be an elite within the Nazi Party, not a mass movement like the SA. The initial plan was for the SS to be no more than a bodyguard of 10 men and an officer in each district. Only Berlin would have a unit of double the normal size. By 1926, 75 *Schutzstaffel* had been formed across Germany. The recruits were to be between 25 and 35 years of age, strong, healthy and morally sound, with no criminal record. Most importantly, they owed their loyalty to Adolf Hitler personally, rather than to the Nazi Party. Furthermore, they also adopted the death's head emblem of the *Stosstrupp Adolf Hitler*. Indeed, the new formation, which more than proved itself in its combined role of bodyguards, street fighters and orderlies for mass meetings and

Left: Hitler 'consecrates' a new SA banner while grasping the *Blutfahne* ('Blood banner') in his left hand. The *Blutfahne* was an early Nazi relic, covered in the blood of a Nazi martyr from the failed putsch.

propagandists, soon become the repository for much potent Nazi symbolism.

As proof of the importance Hitler placed upon the SS, an organisation that he felt maintained the true values of the Nazi Party, he entrusted the *Blutfahne* to its keeping. This both greatly enhanced the prestige of the SS and considerably irritated the SA. Indeed, although the SS was nominally part of the SA, the relationship between the two organisations was uneasy. The SA resented the elitism and intimate relationship between the SS and the party leadership. It was for this reason that the SA leadership ensured that the SS often had to perform the more demeaning political tasks, such as distributing party literature and selling subscriptions to the party newspaper. The SA also ensured that the SS remained vastly smaller than its parent institution and SS membership had declined from about 1000 to 280 by 1929. A series of old Nazi stalwarts struggled to protect the SS from SA interference but, up until 1929, the SS remained largely dominated by the SA.

THE NAZI ACCESSION

In the meantime, Hitler strove for power by legal means. The late 1920s led to an upturn in German economic fortunes and thus were lean times for the Nazi Party. Unemployment fell below one million for the first time since World War I and much of the Nazis' lower middle-class support profited from this and turned away from the extremist party. In the election of 1928, the NSDAP polled 810,000 votes out of the 31 million cast. This was a mere 2.6 per cent of the vote, nowhere near enough to seriously challenge for a place in the government. To quote historian Matthew Hughes: 'Germany no longer needed the Nazis, and in the sort of Darwinian world of struggle and survival of the fittest that the Nazis were so keen to promote, they were about to be made extinct.'

In 1929, however, the New York Stock Exchange on Wall Street crashed, creating serious economic depression in the United States. The shock waves soon spread to Europe and Germany. The American banks recalled the loans that had helped support the German economy in the late 1920s. Unemployment

began to rise rapidly again, eventually reaching five million. There were strikes and running battles in the streets between the Communists and the SA. The recession impacted on all classes and suddenly people once again began to look for more radical solutions. Both the Communists and the Nazis thrived in these circumstances. To German industrialists and conservative politicians, the Nazis were infinitely preferable to the Communists and hence they provided them with vital financial backing. Just as important, if not more so, was the support of the German middle classes.

Nazi Victory

The Nazi Party's fortunes revived dramatically and suddenly. In September 1930, it polled 6,371,000 votes and jumped from 12 to 107 seats in the German parliament, the Reichstag. By 1932, the Nazi vote had more than doubled to 13,732,779 and the party gained 230 Reichstag seats. Hitler's message of radical solutions to Germany's misery was put across to the public through skilful propaganda campaigns. Although the Nazi Party's support dipped slightly later that year in a subsequent election, Hitler and the Nazis had demonstrated that they had considerable popular support. Germany's conservative elite – the industrialists, the landowners or Junkers in the East, and the generals in the *Reichswehr* – decided to turn to Hitler and the NSDAP and give him and his party the opportunity to form part of the government.

They were certain that they could control this Austrian upstart, but they were very rapidly proved wrong. On 30 January 1933, Adolf Hitler became Chancellor of Germany. He had achieved this legally within the democratic system and almost at once he began to dismantle that democracy.

On 6 January 1929, Hitler appointed 28-year-old Heinrich Himmler head of the *Schutzstaffel*, or *Reichsführer der SS*. A prim, unprepossessing man who had been too young to serve in World War I, Himmler had joined the NSDAP in 1923. He rose steadily through the ranks of the party and subsequently the

Left: Hitler marches through a Bavarian town in company with other Nazis. Hess, who helped Hitler write *Mein Kampf*, is on the right of the picture in a light jacket, and directly behind him is none other than Heinrich Himmler.

Below: Himmler and the Old Guard of the SS in Munich in 1933. Himmler ensured the SS played a key role in the elimination of Hitler's enemies both inside and outside of the Nazi party, earning the Führer's gratitude.

Above: Ernst Röhm leaves a Party meeting followed by his nemesis. Röhm's ambitions for the SA, which he saw as his own private army, led to his death in 1934 during the purge of the SA, called the 'Night of the Long Knives'.

SS, and eventually became deputy leader. So, when Erhardt Heiden resigned, Hitler approved Himmler's accession. This appointment was the basis of Himmler's eventual position of tremendous power.

The SA leadership assumed that Himmler would be as easy to overawe as his predecessors. Heinrich Himmler, however, was a man of great energy and drive. Despite still having to carry out heavy propaganda duties, he devoted himself to expanding and reforming the SS. Himmler scrapped the old 10-man system in each district and introduced a military-style structure similar to the SA. He also introduced racial guidelines for SS recruits, tightened discipline and set about expanding the organisation. Fascinated by Germanic and Nordic legend and history, he also ensured that ancient runic script was widely used in SS heraldry. The most famous example was the double Sig-rune, which was famously used on the SS collar patch.

The SS now grew steadily; it reached 1000 members by 1930. A year later, this number had trebled. By contrast, SA membership exploded. The SA never possessed the same aspirations to elite status as that of the SS; it was much more a mass movement. It also had many unruly elements who resented much of the largely Bavarian NSDAP leadership. The Berlin SA rebelled against the appointment of Joseph Goebbels as party *gauleiter* (chief), whose brief specifically included the expulsion of anti-Hitler elements from the capital's NSDAP and SA. Despite the best efforts of Ernst Röhm, who had returned to head the SA in 1930, the rebellion spread throughout the north of Germany. The SS remained totally loyal throughout the crisis, which eventually petered out through lack of financial support.

In return, Hitler increased the responsibility of the SS, not only defining its role as the *Elitetruppe* (elite troops) of the Nazi Party, but also making it the movement's *Polizeidienst* (police service). This largely involved regulating the activities of the SA, essentially ensuring that the more revolutionary elements of the SA did not, in Robert Koehl's words, 'go off half-cocked and thus jeopardis[e] the long term revolutionary aims of the leadership'. This often involved searching the SA for concealed weapons, something which only added to the increasing bitterness between the two groups.

The SS continued to grow within the confines of an ever-expanding SA. SS membership increased more than five times from 10,000 to 50,000 in 1932. During this period, a number of key figures in the history of the *Waffen-SS* and *Totenkopf* entered the SS. Reinhard Heydrich joined in 1932. Heydrich moved upwards through the SS hierarchy at an astronomical pace, and eventually became Himmler's deputy. Two years previously, the most important personality in the story of the *Totenkopf* Division, Theodor Eicke, transferred into the SS from the Ludwigshafen SA. The two men were significant figures in the SS after Hitler came to power, and there was no love lost between them. Nonetheless, both rose rapidly with the SS and, by the time Hitler came to power, Eicke held the rank of *SS-Oberführer*. The rank of *SS-Oberführer* had no direct equivalent in the British, American or German armies. It was a special rank between the ranks of *Standartenführer* (colonel) and *Brigadeführer* (brigadier).

Himmler's reforms and reorganisation ensured that the SS played a crucial role in Hitler's very rapid consolidation of power and elimination of his rivals both outside and inside the party. On 28 February 1933, less than a month after the Nazi accession to power, the Reichstag building burnt to the ground. The Nazis blamed the Communists and Hitler issued a decree giving police powers to the SA and SS. The SA and SS were issued with firearms and started to round up Communists and other possible opponents of the regime. So many were arrested that the prison system could not hold them and the first concentration camps were rapidly built. The removal of the Communist deputies from the Reichstag gave the Nazis and their allies a majority in parliament and allowed Hitler to dismantle the German constitution, ban all other parties and institute a one-party state. Himmler would ensure that the SS became one of the key institutions of this state. Almost at once, the traditional army guard on the Chancellery building was replaced by an SS guard, known as the *Leibstandarte Adolf Hitler*.

With Communist and parliamentary opposition gone, Hitler perceived that the main threat to Nazi rule came from inside the party. Although the German Army was probably the one outside force that might be capable of overthrowing Nazi rule, it was unlikely to do so unless seriously provoked. However, a key Nazi organisation and its leaders seemed to be doing just that. By eliminating the threat that this organisation posed, Hitler would also remove the one centre of power within the Nazi party that remained outside his complete control.

RÖHM'S THREAT TO HITLER

The galvanising effect of Röhm's return to the leadership of the SA and its massive expansion in the first years of the 1930s had increased Hitler's unease towards his erstwhile friend and the organisation that had been so key to Nazi success. The SA had always been the most 'socialist' of the National Socialist Party's various arms and organisations. Indeed, soon after the Nazi accession to power, Röhm was making speeches to massed rallies of the SA talking of the need for a 'second revolution' and claiming that: 'The National Socialist struggle has been a Socialist Revolution. It has been a revolution of the workers' movement. Those who made this revolution must be the ones to speak up for it.' Röhm was clearly implying that he and the SA were the ones to carry the Nazi revolution forwards. Such talk was a considerable embarrassment for Hitler, who had assiduously courted Germany's financiers, industrialists and landowners in his bid for power. This was another bone of contention, as many in the SA disliked his intimate relationship with such groups. Although members of the SA were hardly reformist by inclination, Hitler could not fail to be embarrassed by such rhetoric.

The most serious point of dispute, however, was Röhm's military ambitions for the SA. Ideally, Hitler wanted to retain Röhm's support, but the SA leader's attitude towards the *Reichswehr* forced Hitler to choose between his friend and the institution whose loyalty he required perhaps more than any other if his aspirations for a Greater Germany were to come to fruition. Röhm had long demanded that his storm troopers gain a prominent role within Germany's armed forces and he had aspirations to command the *Reichswehr*. In February 1934, Röhm claimed that the SA was the true army of National Socialism and that the regular army should limit itself to training duties. He also said that the Ministry of Defence should be reorganised, the implication being that he should be at its head. Understandably, the German military leadership was alarmed by such talk. The thought of admitting Röhm's unruly street fighters into the army en masse horrified them. Moreover, the possibility of being commanded by Röhm, a notorious homosexual with a weakness for young men – as he said himself, 'I am an immature and wicked man' – and limited regular military experience, was beyond contemplation.

Hitler's response was to tell Röhm and the SA that this was out of the question and instruct them that the SA's role would be limited to training under the Army's supervision. The Army was delighted and, while Röhm fumed, the Defence Minister General Blomberg demonstrated the Army's loyalty to Hitler by dismissing all non-Aryans and adding the Nazi

eagle and swastika to its uniform, thus politicising an erstwhile non-political organisation.

Yet the SA remained a potent force in German politics. Röhm's SA was 4.5 million–strong; the *Reichswehr* – limited by the World War I peace settlement – contained a mere 100,000 men. Hitler also knew that such a large organisation remained important to the party and that some sort of resolution was required. He first tried to reason with his old friend, telling Röhm that he ought to: 'Forget the idea of a Second Revolution. Believe me, don't cause any trouble.' Yet he sent all 4.5 million SA on leave throughout July 1934.

Quite apart from the threat the SA posed to the Nazi Party, the one man who would profit most from the demise of the influence of Röhm was the *SS-Reichsführer* Heinrich Himmler. The SS, now about 80,000-strong, remained part of the SA; Himmler craved independence. Himmler maintained some feeling for his superior and old comrade Röhm, however, and therefore passed on the task of undermining the SA to his deputy, Reinhard Heydrich. Heydrich at once began to spread rumours of SA plots to seize power and collected and fabricated documents to support these rumours. Although Hitler was already probably inclined to settle the problem once and for all, Himmler and Heydrich did their utmost to force him into decisive action. The two SS men provided Hitler with plenty of 'evidence' of SA misbehaviour and, more seriously, a forthcoming SA rising in Berlin. Eventually, he was convinced and declared that 'I've had enough. I shall make an example of them.' On 28 June 1934, he ordered the elimination of the SA leadership.

RÖHM ARRESTED

Two days later, Hitler himself, with a number of SS men from the *Leibstandarte* commanded by Sepp Dietrich, arrested Röhm and much of the national SA

Right: A Party rally at Nuremberg after Röhm's death in 1934. In the centre is Hitler, with Himmler on his right and Victor Lutze, Röhm's successor as head of the purged SA, on his left.

leadership at Bad Weissee. Meanwhile, in Berlin, the rest of *Leibstandarte*, supported by the newly-formed concentration camp guard detachments under Theodor Eicke, rounded up SA men and other rivals. It was measure of the confidence that the Nazi and SS leadership had in Eicke that he was entrusted with the task of dealing with Röhm.

Hitler decided at some point during 1 July to have the SA leader killed. Himmler, as a chief organiser of the purge, telephoned Eicke, who was by now at the SS offices in Munich, and told him to go and shoot Röhm, who was being held in Munich's Stadelheim prison. Hitler, however, had demanded that his old friend first be allowed to commit suicide and Eicke

Above: The concentration camp at Dachau was established on 20 March 1933. Under Theodor Eicke's management, it became the model on which the entire camp system was based.

was ordered to give Röhm the opportunity to take his own life.

Eicke, accompanied by his adjutant *SS-Sturmbannführer* (Major) Michael Lippert and *SS-Gruppenführer* (Lieutenant-General) Heinrich Schmauser, the local SS liaison officer with the army, set off for the prison. The prison governor Robert Koch refused to hand Röhm over without the correct paperwork. Koch called the Minister of Justice, Hans Frank, to ask for

Röhm that he had 10 minutes to come to a decision. Eicke, Lippert and Schmauser withdrew to the corridor. They waited for 15 minutes and then Eicke and Lippert re-entered the cell, pistols drawn. Eicke told Röhm: 'Chief of Staff, make yourself ready!' Röhm replied, 'Aim slowly and carefully.' Eicke and Lippert fired simultaneously. Röhm slumped to the floor gasping, 'My Führer! My Führer!' Eicke responded, 'You should have thought of that earlier; it's too late now.' It took a third bullet administered at close range to finish the SA leader off as he lay wounded on the floor.

Estimations of the number murdered during the purge vary. Hitler admitted to 77 victims in a speech to the Reichstag on 13 July 1934, yet historians set the figure anywhere between a hundred or more to a

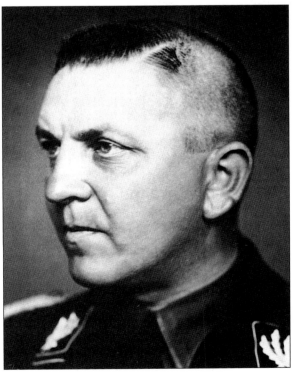

orders, but Eicke grabbed the telephone receiver from the governor and yelled at the startled Minister that he had no business interfering as he, Eicke, had been given specific instructions by Hitler. Frank, apparently reassured by this, told Koch not to hinder Eicke any more.

EICKE'S ROLE IN RÖHM'S DEATH

The three SS men then made their way to Röhm's cell. There Eicke told Röhm: 'You have forfeited your life! The Führer gives you a last chance to avoid the consequences.' He left a loaded pistol and a copy of the party newspaper *Völkische Beobachter*, which contained details of the purge, in the room and told

Above: Theodor Eicke, the man who shaped, organised and led the *Totenkopf* Division until his death in 1943. An energetic and ambitious man, he rose rapidly through the SS, despite clashes with Himmler.

thousand. Whatever the case, it broke the power of the SA as a rival to Hitler.

The organisation was reduced from four million to just over one million and stripped of its weapons. It never regained the influence it had once held. By contrast, Himmler and the SS profited immensely from the purge. On 26 July 1934, the *Völkische Beobachter* announced that 'in consideration of [its] very meritorious service', the SS was elevated to the 'standing of an independent organisation within the NSDAP'. Himmler had finally gained his autonomy and his organisation's ascendancy within Nazi Germany was ensured. Himmler, who had held the title of *Reichsführer-SS* for five years, finally was just that. He was finally only directly subordinate to Hitler. Also, contrary to Hitler's earlier promise to the Army that it and the Navy would be the only armed organisations, Hitler gave the SS permission to form armed units.

The SS had gained much from the Night of the Long Knives and so, too, did Theodor Eicke. Himmler's high opinion and trust in Eicke were well demonstrated by his being given the task of killing Röhm. Indeed, Eicke's role in the purge proved to be a turning point in his career. The rewards came quickly. Only four days after the murder, Himmler appointed Eicke Inspector of Concentration Camps and Leader of SS Guard Formations (*Inspekteur der Konzentrationlager und Führer der SS-Wachverbände*). This was a new SS office and with it came promotion. On 11 July 1934, Eicke was promoted to *SS-Gruppenführer*, the second highest commissioned rank in the organisation.

EICKE AND THE CAMP SYSTEM

Before discussing Eicke's new responsibilities, it is worth examining his early career within the Nazi concentration camp system. As the prison system had struggled to contain the vast numbers of political prisoners arrested in the wake of the Reichstag fire and subsequent legislation banning all opposition to the Nazi party, the SS and SA set up a number of concentration camps to hold the overflow. Himmler established the camp at Dachau on 20 March 1933.

Right: At first propaganda was used to show the outside world that life in the camps was not harsh. Here a guard gives one of the inmates a cigarette. Such generosity would not last long after the cameras had gone.

Himmler sacked its first commandant, Hilmar Wäckerle, over the murder of a number of prisoners in his care. The Reichsführer appointed Eicke in Wäckerle's place, but this did not mean the institution of a more liberal regime. Eicke immediately undertook a number of administrative reforms at the camp and, in place of the casual and random brutality of Wäckerle's regime, instituted a more organised structure of abuse for the inmates, one which became a model for the whole concentration camp system.

His elaborate system of regulations for the treatment of prisoners and disciplinary and punishment codes for the 'Maintenance of Discipline and Order' (*zur Aufrechterhaltung der Zucht und Ordnung*) were issued on 1 October 1933. These codes laid out the offences for which a prisoner could be punished and the severity of the punishment. Punishment ranged from the death penalty for a long list of crimes including political agitation, mutiny or attempted escape, down to solitary confinement on bread-and-water rations or merely suspension of mail privileges for more minor infringements. Eicke also introduced a formalised system of corporal punishment (*Prügelstrafe*), although more casual violence such as kicks and punches from the guards still continued. This corporal punishment usually took the form of whippings, commonly 25 lashes, although staking out prisoners and similar practices also occurred.

The whippings were carried out at Eicke's specific orders in the presence of the camp commandant, the SS staff and the inmates. He rotated the responsibility for administering the punishment among the SS officers, non-commissioned officers (NCOs) and guards. Rudolf Höss, later the commandant of Auschwitz, was an *SS-Unterscharführer* (corporal) at Dachau in 1934 and witnessed the whipping of two men caught stealing cigarettes:

'The first prisoner, a small impenitent malingerer, was made to lie across the block. Two soldiers held his

head and hands and two block leaders carried out the punishment, delivering alternate strokes. The prisoner uttered no sound. The other prisoner, a professional politician of strong physique, behaved quite otherwise. He cried out at the very first stroke, and tried to break free. He went on screaming to the end, although the commandant told him several times to be quiet. I was stationed in the front rank and was thus compelled to watch the whole procedure. I say

compelled, because if I had been in the rear of the company I would not have looked. When the man began to scream, I went hot and cold all over. In fact the whole thing, even the beating of the first prisoner, made me shudder.'

Eicke would not have approved of Höss's squeamishness (one should remember, however, that Höss supervised the murder of 2.5 million people at Auschwitz) and the specific purpose of the enforced

administration and attendance of these whippings was to harden his SS men. They were to carry out such beatings without flinching. Eicke also insisted that the guards view the prisoners as enemies of the state with an absolute and fanatical hatred. Again, Höss is instructive when recounting the fate of four SS men who were found to be involved in a racket with the prisoners. After personally tearing the SS insignia from the men, Eicke launched into a long speech. Any show of sympathy would be regarded by the 'enemies of state' as weakness, which they would immediately exploit. Furthermore, it was unworthy for an SS man to feel pity for 'enemies of the state'. He had no room for weaklings in his ranks, and if any man felt that way he should withdraw to a monastery as quickly as possible. Only the tough and determined were of any use to him. It was not for nothing that they wore the death's head badge and always kept their weapons loaded!

Above: A camp inmate is welcomed for the benefit of the camera by a camp guard. The camp guards were all members of the SS and were to form the backbone of the *Totenkopf* in its early years.

Above right: Another posed photograph for the consumption of the outside world. Inmates register their details and wait for a medical check under the constant eye of the camp guards.

Thus Eicke demanded that his men were tough and hated their enemy. This was coupled to a disciplinary regime which demanded blind and absolute obedience to superior SS officers. This was a pattern of behaviour that would be repeated by SS men at concentration camps, extermination camps and in combat units throughout World War II.

Eicke's success brought him promotion, although his constant demands for autonomy, better quality

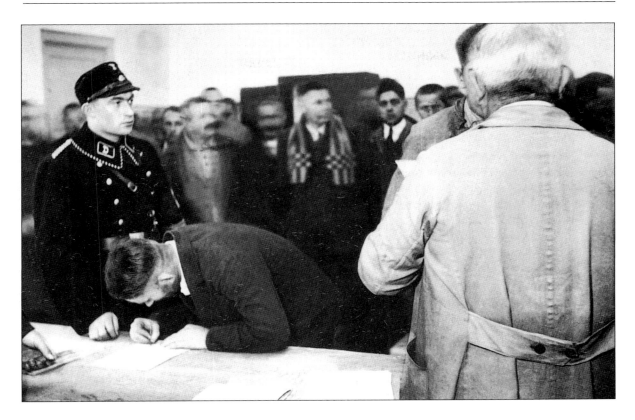

recruits and equipment and weaponry for his men brought him into occasional conflict with his direct superior, Sepp Dietrich, who at that time headed the *SS-Oberabschnitt Süd* (Southern Regional Administrative District). Himmler noticed that Eicke was a rising talent within the SS and subsequently gave him an important role in purge of the SA. As already noted, Eicke's successful participation in the Night of the Long Knives proved a very positive boost to his career in the SS.

As the inspector of the entire concentration camp system, he had responsibility for all administrative matters and each commandant was his direct subordinate. He closed down some of the smaller local camps and concentrated on newer and larger facilities based around four massive camps within Germany – Dachau, Buchenwald, Sachsensausen and Lichtenburg. After Anschluss with Austria in 1938, a camp was constructed at Mauthausen. All the camps

were run on the Dachau model, with the same systems of regulations and punishments. Eicke also introduced the economic activities he had instituted at Dachau across the system. The forced labour undertaken by the inmates proved so successful that, in 1938, Himmler removed the responsibility for this source of income from Eicke and gave it to the *SS-Verwaltungsamt* (SS Administrative Office) under Oswald Pohl. The skill with which Eicke ran the system in the years before World War II demonstrated the man's talents for organisation, motivation and utter ruthlessness, all of which became even more apparent when he led men during war.

THE ARMED-SS AND *TOTENKOPFVERBÄNDE*

Adolf Hitler's bodyguard, the *Leibstandarte*, which in early 1934 consisted of 986 men, had played an important and muscular role in the Röhm purge. As a reward, Hitler promoted its commander, Sepp

Dietrich, to *SS-Obergruppenführer* (General). *Liebstand-arte* was soon converted to a motorised formation, which was a rare honour in 1934, given that the vast majority of the German Army remained horse-drawn. Furthermore, the *Leibstandarte* began to train for specific military tasks and took to wearing field grey.

There were other armed SS units, too. A number of *SS Politische Bereitschaften* (Political Reserve Squads) had also been involved in the Night of the Long Knives. Later that year, Hitler announced that these squads were to be brought together and expanded into a force called the *SS-Verfügungstruppe* (SS-VT – Special Disposal Troops). The SS-VT would consist of three *standarten* – the equivalent of an infantry regiment – each of three battalions and a motorcycle company and a mortar company. Paul Hausser, a former *Reichswehr* general, was recruited to supervise the SS-VT's military training and he established two officer cadet schools at Bad Tölz and Braunschweig. The first *standarte*, later given the honour title *Deutschland*, was formed in Munich and equipped as a horse-drawn infantry regiment. In Hamburg, a second *Standarte*, named *Germania*, was set up soon afterwards. The third and final SS-VT *standarte*, *Der Führer*, was established in 1938, after the *Anschluss* with Austria. Hausser and the officers who accompanied him brought a vigour to the training and equipment of the SS-VT that turned them into remarkably competent 'troops' in a short space of time.

THE *TOTENKOPFVERBÄNDE*

There was a third branch of the armed SS: Eicke's concentration camp guards, or SS-*Totenkopfverbände* (Death's Head Units). By 1936, the concentration camp system was working largely as Eicke had planned, so he turned his attention to the training and equipment of his camp guards. He had weeded the sadists and bullies out of his first command and replaced them with better quality personnel; reliable and disciplined SS officers and men. Eicke originally organised the guards into six battalions, each assigned to the six concentration camps then in existence and named after the region in which they were based: for example, *SS-Oberbayen* guarded Dachau

and *SS-Sachsen* was responsible for the Sachsenburg camp. Hitler's recognition of the SS-VT in September 1935, however, gave Eicke the opportunity to expand his guard units. In March 1936, Himmler agreed to increase the size of Eicke's unit from 1800 to 3500 men. Himmler demanded that the new recruits be between 17 and 22 years old, at least 5 foot 10 inches (178 cm) tall, in good health and of 'racially pure stock'. Such requirements of near physical perfection were not uncommon in early armed SS units; Sepp Dietrich initially demanded that the recruits to *Leibstandarte* Adolf Hitler have no fillings in their teeth, and all members of the SS were expected to be of so-called 'Aryan' extraction. On 29 March, the *Reichsführer-SS* officially designated the concentration guards the *Totenkopfverbände,* and allocated them their distinctive death's head collar patches.

Eicke's men officially came under Oswald Pohl's *SS-Verwaltungsamt* (SS Administrative Office), which in turn was a branch of the *SS-Haupamt* (SS Central Office). The *Verwaltungsamt* was responsible for maintaining and supplying the camp guards and negotiating their budget with the Reich Ministry of Interior. Financing the *Totenkopfverbände* – and the rest of the armed SS for that matter – from this source reassured the army that the SS was not a rival military organisation. The *SS-Haupamt* was also responsible for the *Totenkopfverbände*'s training and indoctrination. In practice, however, Eicke had considerable autonomy, which he used to shape the unit into the elite formation that he desired. Although the *Totenkopf*'s training, organisation and ideological motivation will be examined in depth in the next chapter, it is worth examining briefly here Eicke's philosophy in regard to his concentration camp guards: 'They were the only soldiers who, even in peacetime, faced the enemy every hour of the day and night – the enemy behind the wire.'

According to Eicke, the concentration camps contained the most dangerous enemies of Nazi Germany and he and the *Totenkopfverbände* had been specifically given the task of guarding these enemies by the Führer. This specially selected – racially, politically and physically – group of men was therefore an elite within an elite. Eicke continually sought to convince his men of the 'fact', in the words of historian Charles Sydnor, 'that they served in the most important and finest formation in the SS. Eicke's efforts produced one effect he desired by removing, in the minds of his men, the stigma of the SSTV (SS-*Totenkopfverbände*) as jailers or prison guards.' Simultaneously, as then and the subsequent behaviour of the SSTV suggest, he created an atmosphere conducive to indoctrination in political fanaticism.

HIGHLY DISCIPLINED FORMATION

This process of indoctrination and rigorous training produced a highly disciplined, motivated, first-class paramilitary formation. The men of the

Below: A prisoner is beaten at Dachau. The SS guards were taught by Eicke to hate the inmates and regard them as enemies of the state. Beatings were encouraged by Eicke as a means of brutalising the guards.

Right: Eicke, his face blurred, addresses a new intake of prisoners at Dachau before the war, watched by his guards. The sign on the wall reads, 'You are nothing – your people are everything'.

Totenkopfverbände were largely inured to the infliction of cruelty as a result of the camp regime. They were devoted to Eicke and willing to obey him without question. Himmler, for one, was certainly impressed and showered Eicke and the *Totenkopfverbände* with effusive praise.

In 1937, Eicke reorganised and further centralised the structure of the camp system. He also took the opportunity to expand and reorganise the *Totenkopfverbände*. There were then five *Totenkopfverbände* battalions in existence. Eicke regrouped these into three regiments, which, designated by name and number, were posted to the three enlarged concentration camps at the centre of Eicke's system. SS-*Totenkopfstandarte I Oberbayen* stayed at Dachau. SS-*Totenkopfstandarte II Brandenburg* was based at Sachenhausen near Oranienburg and SS *Totenkopfstandarte III Thüringen* guarded the massive Buchenwald camp at Weimar. After the *Anschluss* with Austria in 1938, in which incidentally *Liebstandarte* and the *SS-Verfügungstruppe Deutschland* and *Germania* regiments took part, Eicke gained a fourth Austrian regiment. In September of that year, SS-*Totenkopfstandarte IV Ostmark* was formed to guard the new Mauthausen camp near Linz.

THE APPROACH OF WAR

As Hitler's foreign policy became increasingly aggressive in the late 1930s, Himmler sought to persuade his leader of the need for an increased role for the armed SS. Himmler argued that the threat of war meant that an expansion of the SS would provide greater internal security. After all, as Himmler himself had said in 1936, the role of the SS was to 'guarantee the security of Germany from the interior, just as the *Wehrmacht* [Defence Power – as the *Reichswehr* was known after 1935] guarantees the safety of the honour, the greatness and peace of the Reich from the exterior.' Hitler was receptive to Himmler's argu-

ments, as he had established complete control of Germany's armed forces – members now swore a personal oath of allegiance to him – and had assumed the role of Supreme Commander. Therefore, Hitler felt that he could now consider the future of his armed SS formations. He promised Himmler that he would legally define their status and purpose.

Hitler issued the relevant decree on 17 August 1938. This stipulated that, for special domestic political tasks or by use of the *Wehrmacht* in the event of mobilisation, the SS-VT, the *SS-Junkerschulen* (SS Officer Cadet Schools) and the SS-*Totenkopfverbände* and its reserve units were to be trained and organised as military units. In peacetime, they were to remain under Himmler's command. For the first time, service in the SS-VT would count towards a person's compulsory military service obligation.

The decree also had certain specific provisions regarding the SS-*Totenkopfverbände*, or Death's Head Units. The *Totenkopfverbände*, as a party organisation, was not part of either the *Wehrmacht* or the police.

Instead, it was a standing armed force of the SS available for any internal purpose that Hitler determined. It also provided a template for the unit's organisation. The *Totenkopfverbände* was divided into four regiments (*Oberbayen*, *Brandenburg*, *Thüringen* and *Ostmark*) of three battalions each. Each battalion was to have three infantry companies and a machine gun company. The units were also to be fully motorised, still a rarity in Germany, even in 1938. The Führer reserved the power to himself make changes to the *Totenkopfverbände*'s strength and organisation.

HIMMLER'S LOOPHOLE

He had, however, left Himmler a loophole which the *Reichsführer* used to increase the size of the *Totenkopfverbände*'s strength still further. The decree had defined the unit's role to be a 'standing armed force of the SS' for use in 'clearing up special tasks of a police nature'. More specifically, this implied the guarding of the concentration camps. However, in event of mobilisation, the *Totenkopfverbände* would be replaced at the camps by older members of the *Allgemeine-SS*. The motorised units, strengthened by its reserves, would thus become a special police force under Himmler's command.

These provisions were soon put to the test. Hitler demanded the annexation of neighbouring Czechoslovakia's Sudentenland region, which had a sizeable German-speaking population, to the Third Reich. The Czechs, whose main line of border fortifications lay in this area and who possessed a formidable and well-equipped army, understandably refused. Hitler ordered the *Wehrmacht* to draw up plans for invasion and ordered the mobilisation of the armed forces and the SS. Himmler instituted a 'police strengthening' emergency order on 15 October 1938, which activated the *Allgemeine-SS* reservists for service in the camps. This order gave Himmler the opportunity to expand the *Totenkopfverbände* beyond the stipulations of Hitler's August decree. He drew on all convenient pools of manpower and, accordingly, in February 1939, SS-VT men whose period of enlistment was nearing its end were given the opportunity to join the *Totenkopfverbände* as NCO candidates. Eicke promised to promote any of these candidates from the SS-VT who proved suitable within three months. Himmler was also allowed to recruit directly from the SA. Furthermore, the Czech crisis also placed *Totenkopfverbände* units under army control for the first time and two battalions of *Totenkopfstandarte I*

Below: NCOs from the *Totenkopfverbände* take a moment to relax and pose for a group photograph during their training. Eicke initially struggled to equip his men, and the *Wehrmacht* refused to provide supplies for them.

Oberbayen crossed the border into Czechoslovakia before the total German takeover to help the Nazi movement in the country prepare for occupation.

FURTHER EXPANSION

The expansion and recruitment drive for the *Totenkopfverbände* proved quite successful. The unit had grown to include *Totenkopfstandarte V Dietrich Eckart*, a medical battalion, an anti-tank demonstration company, a motorised signals platoon and a semi-motorised engineer unit. According to Eicke's own figures, the total strength of *Totenkopfverbände* in mid-1939 stood at 22,033 men (755 officers, 5005 NCOs and 16,273 enlisted men). He also provided an inventory of the unit's weaponry. There were pistols and a gas mask for every man, as well as 19,643 rifles,

325 heavy and 486 light machine guns and 1458 machine pistols. The *Totenkopfverbände* had increased threefold in less than a year. Training and equipping such a large number of new recruits in such a short period of time – and without the *Wehrmacht*'s cooperation – put Eicke under massive pressure.

In May 1939, Hitler fixed the minimum size of the unit at 14,000 men and allowed Himmler to increase its strength to 25,000 in the event of further mobilisation. To ringfence Eicke's men away from the manpower demands of the *Wehrmacht*, Hitler ruled that service in the *Totenkopfverbände* counted as the military obligation of its SS personnel. The conditions of the May decree soon occurred. As war loomed over Poland in August 1939, Himmler issued an emergency call-up of all Death's Head units reservists on the 30th of that month. The Dachau, Buchenwald, Sachsenhausen and Mauthausen concentration camps acted as depots for the *Totenkopfverbände* regiments, which were outfitted and held in readiness to act as police

Above: Taken in 1939, this photograph shows members of the *Totenkopfverbände* being briefed by an officer during training for the invasion of Poland, but they were to see little action in that campaign.

reserves, implying that they would take on occupation duties in event of war.

On 1 September 1939, five German armies invaded Poland and, that morning, the Luftwaffe (the German Air Force) bombed Warsaw. *Leibstandarte* and the SS-VT unit *Deutschland* were both committed to the campaign. *Germania* was held in reserve. The three original *Standarten* – *Oberbayern*, *Brandenburg* and *Thüringen* – were ordered to leave their barracks at Dachau, Sachsenhausen and Buchenwald respectively for a secret assignment in Poland. Hitler had ordered that the three regiments be deployed in army rear areas in the war zone to conduct 'police and security' duties behind German lines. Eicke's Death's Head units were finally going to war.

33

CHAPTER TWO

ORGANISATION

The *Totenkopfverbände* – and later the *Totenkopf* Division itself – were thoroughly drilled and trained by Eicke, who also oversaw recruitment for the unit as it expanded. As the division's fighting reputation increased, it claimed the best equipment the Reich could provide.

'If you answer the call of the *Waffen-SS* and volunteer to join the ranks of the great front of SS divisions, you will belong to a corps which from the very beginning has been associated with outstanding achievements, and therefore has developed an especially deep feeling of comradeship. You will be bearing arms with a corps that embraces the most valuable elements of the young German generation. Above all, you will be especially bound to the National Socialist ideology.' (*Waffen-SS* recruiting pamphlet)

Until 1943, the *Waffen-SS* remained a largely volunteer force and new recruits were left in no doubt that they had joined a unique and elite organisation. Theodor Eicke, as commander of the Death's Head concentration camp guard units, and later the 3rd SS Division *Totenkopf*, went one step further. He told the men under his command that they were more than just SS men; they were an elite within an elite, the very embodiment of National Socialism. Such were Eicke's character and the ideological indoctrination he imposed on his men that the members of *Totenkopf* seem not only to have believed him, but also

Left: A *Totenkopf* officer and despatch rider check their position during training manoeuvres in France, sometime in late 1942. The division's insignia can clearly be seen on their collar patches.

performed acts of outstanding bravery and endurance for him.

PREWAR SELECTION AND RECRUITMENT

The SS had always been an elite group within the National Socialist movement. The early recruits were expected to meet stringent criteria. On 4 October 1932, Himmler established the two fundamental conditions for joining the SS. First, the men who made up the organisation had to be 'tall, fit SS men with excellent racial features, preferably in the bloom of youth'. Secondly, they should be a minimum height 170cm (5ft 7in), not older than 30 and able to provide a medical certificate. As there was a huge influx into both the SA and the SS in 1933 and 1934 after Hitler's accession to power, Himmler was again able to tighten the selection criteria to the SS. The minimum height was raised to 174cm (5ft 8in), the maximum age dropped to 23 and recruits were required to have perfect eyesight. Furthermore, a certificate of good behaviour from the police was required.

These regulations remained in force until 1938, when the massive expansion of the armed SS in preparation for war necessitated a relaxation of these stringent requirements to ensure enough men were recruited. As Himmler decreed in December 1938: 'In the next five years lesser demands are made for all

units of the SS respecting physical defects, if they are not of a eugenic or racial nature.' In 1940, the *Waffen-SS* was forced to adopt the same physical criteria as the Wehrmacht.

Essentially, SS selection criteria rested on racial, physical and character attributes. Intellectual abilities were not high on Himmler's list. During the mustering process, the SS had a five-point scale to evaluate the candidate's racial features, ranging from 'purely Nordic' to 'suspicion of extra-European blood mixtures'. To assess the candidate's physique, there was a nine-point system, which was complemented by tests of strength, endurance, speed and courage. Somewhat in contrast was the 20-minute intelligence

Left: Himmler inspects members of the Austrian SS from the Salzburg region after the *Anschluss* with Austria in 1938. The fourth *Totenkopf* regiment *Ostmark* was formed from Austrians to guard the new Mauthausen camp.

A candidate's political reliability, on the other hand, was of considerable concern. The June 1936 SS regulations stated that the SS should exclude 'those who could not guarantee that they would defend the National Socialist state without question and at all times because of their origins, previous political views or activities'.

This meant that past members of the Communist Party or Social Democratic Party, those from families with such 'unreliable' political sympathies, or those who were masons or theologists were excluded. For units such as the *Totenkopfverbände* and other armed SS formations, proof of 'sound' political credentials was largely ignored. This was because, on the whole, they recruited from the *Allgemeine-SS*, the Reich Labour Service, the Hitler Youth and SA – all Nazi organisations the membership of which indicated at least some sense of National Socialist ardour. Strangely enough, although it was an advantage, membership of the Nazi Party was not a requirement for joining the armed SS. For example, in July 1937, only 28 per cent of the *Totenkopfverbände* were members of the NSDAP.

Within these selection criteria, Himmler tried to establish specific requirements for Eicke's concentration camp guards, declaring in 1936 that the new recruits should be between 17 and 22 years old, at least 178cm (5ft 10in) tall, in good health and of 'racially pure stock'. It was not possible to meet such conditions and fill the expanding Death's Head formations, so that standards had to be relaxed somewhat. Initially, most of the volunteers were slightly older than Himmler had wished, averaging between 25 and 30 years of age. Many were World War I veterans – which brought military experience into the *Totenkopfverbände* – and had moved through the SA or the *Allgemeine-SS* before ending up under Eicke's command. As the expansion continued, however, the average age of recruits began to drop. The

test, which consisted of a three-line dictation, a 'minor comprehension exercise' and three 'small arithmetic problems'. A candidate's intellect was not of great importance, nor was his social background (in contrast to the regular army), although he had to be single, without a criminal record and have not been dishonourably discharged from the army.

Einstellung von

Freiwilligen

für die

SS-Verfügungstruppen
SS-Totenkopfstandarten

Annahmestelle:

Totenkopfverbände offered new opportunities, prestige coupled with the imposing black uniform and the possibility of quick promotion. To some, perhaps, the attraction was the nature of the work involved.

The period of enlistment was initially four years; however, in 1938, it was increased to 12 years. Yet, despite his best efforts, Eicke found that a major obstacle to recruiting was that service in the *Totenkopfverbände* did not count towards the compulsory military service that all young German men faced. Before joining the units, all recruits had to go through a period of conscription in an arm of the services. Although this meant that they would bring basic military skills with them to the *Totenkopfverbände*, not all young Germans were eager for another spell of military-style life once they had completed their national

Above: A recruitment poster asking for volunteers to join either the *SS-Verfügungstruppen* or *SS-Totenkopfverbände*. Both underwent a rapid expansion after the declaration of war in September 1939.

service requirement. It was only in May 1939 that Hitler ordered that service with the formation would count towards the compulsory military requirement.

As Eicke increasingly militarised his Death's Head Units, he continually expressed his disdain for military formalities. In February 1937, he ordered that no 'outdated and useless' practices take place in the *Totenkopfverbände*. He wanted total comradeship in his unit, particularly between company commanders and NCOs. This was not far from Himmler's own concept of unity within the order of the SS. Himmler emphasised the fundamental equality of the SS because he felt that 'the honorary title "SS man" belong[ed] to every active member of the *Schutzstaffel*, from the lowest ranks up to the *Reichsführer-SS*', implying that any difference of rank was a purely practical distinction based on performance. While Himmler stressed the exclusivity of the SS, Eicke stressed the uniqueness of *Totenkopf* within the SS; its superb camaraderie, fidelity and toughness. To Eicke, *Totenkopf* was not part of inferior institutions such as the army, the police or the *SS-Verfügungstruppe*; rather, it was something apart. To emphasise this point, Eicke threatened to transfer to the *Allgemeine-SS* any members who did demonstrate the correct spirit of comradeship or who performed their duties without enthusiasm. Throughout their training, Eicke emphasised the elite nature of the *Totenkopfverbände*, their unrivalled camaraderie and their toughness, and combined this with extremely harsh discipline.

TRAINING

For the SS-*Totenkopfverbände*, basic training took place at the unit's depot at Dachau. The training regime for the armed SS was developed by the retired *Reichswehr* general Paul Hausser, with the help of two experienced officers, Felix Steiner and Cassius Freiherr von Montigny, who later served as Eicke's operations officer. Steiner, a *Stosstrupp* officer in World War I, trained the SS recruits especially for the light infantry role. Together, these men evolved a programme for the SS-VT units *Germania* and *Deutschland*, which Eicke more or less applied to *Totenkopf* when he came to expand its military strength and potential.

The recruit's day started at 0600 hours, with an hour's physical training prior to breakfast. In the morning, the main emphasis usually lay on weapon training. New recruits had to become familiar with their rifles and be able to strip, clean and reassemble

their weapons so expertly that they could reassemble them blindfolded. Lessons also included such basic but important techniques as the clearance of jams and battlefield repairs. Outside the classroom, there was practical instruction on the rifle ranges. After the men had become proficient with weapons, they were taught infantry tactics. The SS instructors placed great emphasis on aggression as a means of overcoming enemy resistance quickly and thus minimising friendly casualties. Techniques of unarmed combat were taught and the recruits later progressed to bayonet fighting. Sport was also central to the curriculum, both as recreation and to increase strength, fitness and endurance. Needless to say, there were regular runs and forced marches with or without full kit. The afternoon would consist of further exercise, cleaning and 'household' tasks, and pressing and repair of uniforms. The evenings were usually the recruits' own. This was

Right: Wilfred Richter joined the SS in 1937 and fought with the *Totenkopf* Division in the Demjansk pocket, where he won the Knight's Cross of the Iron Cross for defending a strongpoint from 16 Russian T-34 tanks in March 1942.

very similar to the regular army's basic training, although there was slightly less emphasis on traditional 'spit and polish' in the SS. The exception to this was the *Leibstandarte*, due to the unit's ceremonial duties.

The SS set great store on the fact that all enlisted men should aspire to become NCOs and all NCOs should aspire to become officers. Equality of opportunity was open to all dependent on ability. In practice, it did not quite work like that. The selection and training of officer candidates began within the home unit. By disregarding selection criteria such as education

and background, the SS platoon commander had considerable freedom in selecting possible officer material. On the positive side, this placed greater emphasis on a possible candidate's soldiering abilities and the equality of opportunity created greater competitiveness among the men. However, the power vested in the SS company and battalion commanders allowed them to exercise bias in favour of their own men at the expense of the greater good of the SS, and they were often guilty of holding on to talented men who passed over for officer training. Himmler in

Left: Arrivals at Auschwitz extermination camp in Poland, where 2.5 million people lost their lives. Its commandant was Rudolf Höss, a former member of the *Totenkopfverbände* under Eicke at Dachau in the 1930s.

April 1938 threatened to 'have regiments inspected by special deputies of my choice to find men suited for leadership functions, because I will have come to the conclusion that the commanders, and unit and company leaders, have not yet understood the importance and the great responsibility [of] this question.'

The situation was not helped by the extremely uneven level of military expertise found among SS officers who had joined the organisation in the early years. Thus the imbalance in military and leadership competence was reflected in the selection of officer candidates. In 1939, the inspector of the SS Junker Cadet Schools Oberführer von Treuenfeld – the SS had two officer training schools at Bad Tölz and Brunswick – found that the level of expertise amongst those sent to the schools was 'extremely' uneven. The following year he estimated that in the previous few years, 40 per cent 'and more' of cadets sent forward 'proved to be unfit'. The Bad Tölz School listed the most serious flaws found amongst candidates: lack of general education and basic military training, lack of previous training as NCOs, applicants overage, lack of motivation, poor infantry skills and basic character defects such as obtuseness, insincerity and indecisiveness. This indicated the selection criteria were not being properly followed at the candidates' parent units. As the demands of the war continued to escalate, the preparatory officer cadet training programme was gradually removed from the parent units and the individual units were required to meet a quota of men to be sent forward to the SS Junker Cadet Schools. Unfortunately, this guaranteed quantity rather than quality.

Once a candidate reached the school, he found himself in an environment not unlike that of army military academies. The course originally lasted 10 months, but this was reduced to four during the war. Candidates were taught military skills such as topography, tactics and combat training, as well as leadership techniques. If a candidate passed, he was forwarded to a two-month platoon leaders' course at Dachau. Once war broke out, this was replaced by a period at an SS or army weapons training school. After this, the candidate was sent back to his unit and promoted to *Untersturmführer* (second lieutenant). Like basic training, the whole process was very similar to traditional army officer training.

There were, however, slight differences in the regime as practised by Eicke on the men of the *Totenkopf* units prior to the outbreak of war. Members spent three weeks out of every month training, with one week of guard duty within the concentration camp. Exposure to the camps, Eicke felt, would reinforce the lessons the *Totenkopf* men had learnt during training – that is, that the inmates were enemies of the Nazi state against whom the SS had to wage an unremitting war. Of course, involvement in concentration camp life also had the hardening effect on *Totenkopf* men that Eicke desired.

POLITICAL INDOCTRINATION

The real difference between army and SS training was the stress placed on political indoctrination within the SS. This was a key part of basic training and at least half the curriculum at the SS Junker Cadet School was devoted to National Socialist ideology. Eicke certainly believed that political indoctrination was possibly the most important part of an SS man's training. In 1937, he appointed a chief education officer to the staff of the concentration camp inspectorate and placed an education officer in each battalion of the *Totenkopfverbände* to conduct daily political training. The men attended several political lectures a week. This training divided into three broad areas: the history of the NSDAP and an examination of the party's programme; the racial beliefs of the SS with special attention paid to those of the *Totenkopfverbände* and, finally, a careful analysis of the enemies of National Socialism. These enemies were, in order of importance, the Jews, freemasonry, Bolshevism and the Church. Initially, Eicke relied on SS indoctrination journals, but he soon found these too bland and relied on his own instinct and somewhat cruder views

to teach members of the *Totenkopfverbände* what he saw as the correct outlook.

Eicke launched a strident anti-religion campaign within the formation. Since the churches were judged to be enemies of National Socialism, he decided to put considerable pressure on members of the *Totenkopfverbände* to renounce their faith. A circular from Eicke in 1940 expressed his personal hatred of Christianity in no uncertain terms:

'Prayer books are things for women and those who wear panties. We hate the stink of incense; it destroys the German soul as Jews destroy the race. We believe in God, but not in his son, for that would be idolatrous and paganistic. We believe in our Führer and the greatness of our Fatherland. For these and nothing else we will fight. If we must therefore die, then not with "Mary pray for us". We will depart as freely as we have lived. Our last breath: "Adolf Hitler!"'

Such was the effect of the campaign that, by 1936, a substantial majority of his men had indeed rejected their churches. Occasionally this resulted in the

estrangement of recruits from their parents and Eicke responded by opening his home to those who fell out with their parents and wanted to spend time with a family.

Such a gesture was typical of Eicke, as he strove to maintain and enhance the camaraderie of *Totenkopf.* He was convinced that esprit de corps could make a unit invincible. He therefore introduced a number of novel practices unheard of within a traditional army unit. He ordered unmarried officers to eat some meals with their men in the enlisted men's mess. He led by example by spending long hours drinking with young *Totenkopf* recruits in the enlisted men's canteen. Eicke went out of his way to make himself available to his men and would often speak to them away from their officers. In February 1937, he installed suggestion boxes in all the camps to which only he had the keys. This gave all members of the *Totenkopfver-bände* direct access to their commander.

Another aspect of Eicke's command which did so much to shape the complexion of *Totenkopf* was his propensity to dismiss or transfer those who did not conform. Any man he felt guilty of disobedience or incompetence, or who incurred his displeasure, was transferred to the *Allgemeine-SS* or the police, or, if this failed, to an unpleasant post within the concentration camp system. He constantly exhorted his officers to root out from the ranks those who did not measure up and there were frequent dismissals and transfers from the unit.

MANPOWER AND REPLACEMENT PROBLEMS

Totenkopf had expanded considerably in the 1930s, but the demands of war put ever greater strains on the division to maintain reasonable levels of manpower. The first major enlargement of *Totenkopf* came in October 1939, when Hitler authorised the creation of three SS divisions: the *Verfügungs* Division based around the SS-VT regiments, the *Polizei* Division created from recruits from the *Ordnungspolizei* and, finally, *Totenkopf*. Meanwhile, *Leibstandarte* was expanded to the size of a large motorised regiment. The new *Waffen-SS* (as the armed SS had now officially become) formations were designated motorised divisions. The motorisation of German divisions was far from complete in 1940 and, right through until the end of the war, most Wehrmacht infantry divisions relied on horse-drawn transport and the soldiers' boots. Thus in theory this placed the new SS divisions amongst the best-equipped German units, although actually getting hold of the transport from a resentful German army was often easier said than done.

Eicke withdrew to Dachau with his staff to form and equip his new division. Although the new *Totenkopf* Division was based roughly on the standard army motorised division, Eicke established three motorised infantry regiments instead of the regular army divisional establishment of two. All this needed

more men. The three *SS-Totenkopfverbände standarte* formed the basis of the three motorised infantry regiments. *SS Heimwehr Danzig* provided most of the men for the artillery regiment. To further support Eicke's division, Himmler established a replacement battalion for each *Totenkopf* regiment within the concentration camp system. There was also a replacement company for each battalion. This meant that, hopefully, Eicke would have plenty of well-trained men to fall back on when *Totenkopf* began to sustain casualties.

The French campaign was more costly for *Totenkopf* than might have been anticipated, with losses running to about 10 per cent of the division's strength. The campaign proved that the *Waffen-SS*

Below: Young *Totenkopfverbände* members in 1938. Eicke had rapidly increased the number of concentration camp guards and was in the process of turning them into an efficient military formation.

Right: SS officer cadets from the SS *Junkerschule* at Bad Tölz on a route march in 1942. Drill was used to instil a sense of discipline and order in the cadets, who would be sent as replacements to any of the *Waffen-SS* divisions.

divisions were decent combat formations, and Hitler therefore gave Himmler permission to double the number of SS divisions from three to six. Part of this process, however, caused a considerable diminution of Eicke's power, as Himmler wanted to free the *Totenkopfverbände* in the concentration camp system for use as a manpower pool for all of the *Waffen-SS* and not just the *Totenkopf* Division. Thus Eicke lost control over the replacements that he received – he was now in the same position as the other *Waffen-SS* divisional commanders and had to take the recruits he was sent by Gottlob Berger, head of the *Waffen-SS* Recruiting Office (*Ergänzungsamt der Waffen-SS*).

EICKE VETS RECRUITS

Eicke, true to character, did not take this quietly. He was extremely worried about dilution of the racial purity of his division. As the *Waffen-SS* expanded, standards began to relax. Eicke was horrified and seemed to believe that the central authorities of the SS were trying to curb his power by sending him undesirable replacements and thus undermine the elite nature of *Totenkopf*. Therefore, throughout the summer of 1940, he was involved in a running battle with Berger's office over the quality of the men that he was being sent. He constantly complained that he was being sent criminals and racial inferiors, and told the division's training officer and racial 'expert' Dr Wilhelm Fuhrländer to carefully vet new recruits for any racial impurities. Eicke also told his unit commanders to screen their men for criminal records.

As a consequence, Eicke rejected 500 of the 700 replacements sent. The only reason he gave was that these men were not wanted because they were racial inferiors or obvious criminal elements. Berger was absolutely exasperated by Eicke's actions – after all, recruits had already been racially examined when they were tested upon joining the SS. Eicke was ordered to stop his examinations, although he

promptly and fallaciously claimed that he had no such policy. He does, however, seem to have won on the issue because, as a member of the SS old guard, he was given perhaps more leeway by his superiors than most divisional commanders. He was eventually given replacements matching his criteria. Eicke may have won the battle, but he eventually lost the war, as the SS leadership managed to sever his links with the concentration camp system in the meantime.

The constant attrition of the unit during the Russian campaign caused Eicke innumerable problems. As the Russian winter began to draw in, Eicke surveyed his battered division, which had been involved in some particularly bitter fighting around Lake Ilmen. He reckoned that the division had suffered 8993 casualties since 24 June, only half of which had been replaced. He was not happy about the quality of these replacement men either, who, in his eyes,

were not of the same high quality as the men that they replaced. Part of this was due to poor training of the replacement officers, whose inexperience soon resulted in their deaths in action. The other problem as Eicke saw it was the inferior moral and physical strength of the ethnic Germans (*volkdeutsche*), whom he claimed were more likely to fall asleep on duty and had a higher propensity for self-inflicted wounds. What angered him most, however, was the lack of

Left: Training at Bad Tölz. The SS put a premium on physical prowess at the expense of intellectual ability or general education. Political education was ensured by feeding candidates a steady stream of propaganda.

Three-quarters of the men assigned to the new division needed to be fully trained and Eicke, as ever, was unhappy about the quality of his new manpower. Thus he pleaded with Himmler that the division should not be returned to combat before these men were properly and intensively trained.

The division lost a significant proportion of its armour at the battle of Kursk in the summer of 1943 and, despite becoming the 3rd SS Panzer Division in October of that year, major rebuilding and replacement of casualties did not occur until the spring and

political indoctrination; there was none of the fanatical zeal that he expected.

The situation only became worse. In the wake of the Soviet winter offensive of 1942, *Totenkopf* was cut off in the Demyansk pocket and had to endure terrible attrition. Himmler had largely allowed this to occur as he had written the original division off and was planning to reconstitute *Totenkopf* as a new panzer grenadier formation. The expanded and re-equipped division needed more men given the losses of 1942. The basis of the new division was the SS Regiment No. 9, which was renamed *Thule*, with a core of 500 men. Six thousand men were transferred into the division from the Labour Service, as well as 1500 reservists and concentration camp men. The new tank regiment drew on personnel from the SS Mountain Division *Nord*. To these were added the shattered remains of the division, which was finally withdrawn from the Eastern Front in October 1942.

early summer of 1944. During May and June 1944, the front in ahead of *Totenkopf* in Romania was reasonably quiet and Himmler took the opportunity to try to make good the losses of a winter's hard fighting. New consignments of equipment, weapons, vehicles and spare parts arrived and, more importantly, Himmler sent 6000 men to the division. Admittedly, 1500 of these were *Totenkopf* men on leave or recovering from wounds, but Himmler did divert 4500 recruits from 16th SS Panzer Grenadier Division *Reichsführer-SS*. Thus *Totenkopf* was in reasonable

Below: A pre-war picture of *SS-Totenkopfstandarte II Brandenburg* during training in the snow. Later experience in the Soviet Union during the war led to the issue of reversible camouflaged winter clothing.

condition to face the forthcoming Soviet summer offensive. Yet this was the last major influx of men that *Totenkopf* would enjoy before the end of the war.

DISCIPLINE

Readying *Totenkopf* for the forthcoming Western campaign meant bringing in new men. Not all of them were from Eicke's rigorously trained and indoctrinated concentration camp empire. Of the 15,000 men who made up the original *Totenkopf* Division, only 7000 were from the pre-war *Totenkopfverbände*. The rest were drawn from the *Allgemeine-SS*, the *Ordungspolizei* and the newer, less well trained and disciplined *Totenkopf* formations set up in the last weeks before war broke out. To install a proper sense of order among these men, Eicke imposed a draconian

Left: Officer cadets attend a lecture at the SS *Junkerschule* Bad Tölz. The curriculum contained a range of military skills such as leadership, topography and basic staffwork, and a large dose of indoctrination.

set of rules and regulations. The penalties for even a minor infringement were extremely harsh. For the crime of disobeying a specific order, an officer would be transferred back to guard duties in the concentration camp system. This became standard *Totenkopf* Division practice throughout the war. Eicke, however, was capable of much worse.

EICKE'S HARSH PUNISHMENTS

When, in November 1939, six men based at Dachau stole a truck, indulged in a night out in Munich and collided with a tram on the way back to the camp, Eicke decided to make an example of them. He stripped them of their rank and sent them to Buchenwald concentration camp as inmates for an indefinite period. This was technically illegal, as Eicke had no right to imprison his men in the camps for infringements of the military code. The fact that no one noticed or challenged his action, however, meant that he could employ such means for dealing with troublemakers for some months to come. As a substantial proportion of his men had already served in the camps as guards, they were extremely aware of what a terrible punishment this was. Eicke also threatened to have shot anyone who stole or used a vehicle for unauthorised purposes in the future.

Eicke subsequently used the threat of incarceration in the camps in a quite indiscriminate manner. The day after the truck-stealing incident, a private requested a transfer out of the division so that he could resign from the SS. His argument, which was perfectly legal, was that he had already served his compulsory military service obligation in the army. Eicke had the unfortunate man expelled from the SS, dressed in a camp uniform, paraded in front of the entire division and then shipped off to Buchenwald. Thus Eicke used the threat of the camps as a disciplinary tool and also to ensure that the disgruntled members of his division stayed where they were. Any

men who might have hoped for a transfer resigned themselves to staying with *Totenkopf*. The success of Eicke's measures is borne out by the fact that there were no more requests for transfer or offers of resignation. Furthermore, the discipline problems that had plagued *Totenkopf* upon the influx of new personnel lessened drastically.

Although Eicke remained unhappy with many of the new recruits that he received, it was clear that the conflicting manpower demands of the *Wehrmacht* and the *Waffen-SS* meant that he could not just send every problem case back to the concentration camps. Thus he came up with a more practical method of punishment by creating a penal section, or *Sonderkommando*, for the engineer battalion. As such, these men would perform the more dirty, unpleasant and, once division went into combat, dangerous tasks. If a man was sentenced to a period in prison, Eicke would simply expel him from the SS, then commute the man's sentence and transfer him to the penal battalion for an indefinite period of time.

Nonetheless, like all formations, during periods of relative inactivity out of the line, *Totenkopf* had its share of discipline problems. Eicke's methods of dealing with these breaches, as the above examples have already proved, did not conform to the usual methods. Even by SS – and certainly by German Army – standards, Eicke's methods of enforcing discipline were, to say the least, robust. The standards of morality that he applied to the disciplinary infractions of members of the *Totenkopf* are even more telling.

By December 1939, a regular system of courts martial was in place for *Totenkopf*, thus removing much of the responsibility for the trial and sentencing from Eicke personally. That is not to say, however, that his subordinates were any more lenient. Eicke introduced to the division the same system of 'sharp arrest' punishments that he had used in the concentration camp system. 'Sharp arrest' for *Totenkopf* meant exactly the same as it had in the camps – up to 30 days solitary confinement with rations reduced to two pieces of bread and a litre of water daily, supplemented by one warm meal every fourth day. Eicke's intention was to prevent further offences by always sentencing harshly on the first offence and thereby ensuring his men did not become persistent trouble-makers. In his study of the division, Charles Sydnor cites a number of examples of extremely harsh penalties for first-time offenders: 'Many men received stiff sentences ranging from several-days' to three-weeks confinement for such things as smoking in the motor pool, returning a few hours late from leave, or getting drunk while off duty. One SS soldier was sentenced to two weeks of solitary confinement for committing adultery with the wife of another SS man.' Indeed, Eicke specified that a man should spend one day in solitary confinement for each hour he returned late from leave. If he was 24 or more hours late from leave, he would be automatically court-martialled.

The men of the division indulged in their fair share of brawling in nearby Stuttgart, a railway junction packed with off-duty *Wehrmacht* troops. The local *Wehrmacht* field commander complained to Eicke that drunken gangs of *Totenkopf* men roamed the city, picking fights with *Wehrmacht* personnel and relieving them of their side arms. Only one man from the division, however, was ever charged with brawling. This was when an officer, while blind drunk, shot up a hotel bar. Eicke paid for the damage and promptly relieved the officer of his command, sending him back to the inspectorate of concentration camps for a new assignment. When redeployed to Kassel in Westphalia in early 1940, Himmler, determined that *Totenkopf* make a good impression, told Eicke to clamp down on the units drinking in the town. In response, Eicke banned all visits to bars and restaurants in Kassel. Any drinking would in future be done in the division's canteens.

These lists of offences, most little more than misdemeanours, are not shown to give the impression that *Totenkopf* was particularly undisciplined. Far from it, Eicke's division seems in fact no worse and a considerable sight better behaved than most formations. What these examples do illustrate however, is Eicke's uncompromising approach to discipline and his belief that his men should obey his orders without question. When the division expanded he received an influx of men who did not come up to the standard

Above: Prewar *Totenkopfverbände* members on a training exercise armed with the Mauser Gewehr 98. Their white helmets are unusual: this practice was only widely adopted by the Germans in the winter of 1941.

of his hardened and disciplined core of pre-*Totenkopfverbände* veterans, so he set about transforming them through a mixture of rigorous training and absolutely unbending discipline. By and large, he

succeeded; there seem to have been very little discontent within the division. Sydnor notes the case of an artillery private who wrote to his previous employer complaining about the conditions he endured. The division's censors passed the letter on to Eicke, who promptly dismissed the man and told the rest of the division that any future occurrences of such disloyalty would be considered treasonable. This does, however, seem to have been an isolated case.

Once the division began to experience the war in earnest, Eicke's singular attitude to discipline became even more evident. As an example, the officer who massacred British prisoners of war at La Paradis during the French campaign went unpunished (this incident is dealt with in more detail in the next chapter). Clearly Eicke did not view this sort of thing in quite the same light as smoking in the motor pool or requesting a transfer. This attitude became quite

property. An SS man convicted of attempted rape had his punishment of two years in prison changed to an equal sentence in the penal company. Similar treatment was accorded to an SS private convicted of public drunkenness, rape and the severe beating of an elderly French woman. It is clear that Eicke did not consider these acts of violence against the enemy civilian population as particularly serious.

Totenkopf officers who mistreated French civilians often received even lighter punishment, such as an official warning. Two lieutenants stole a large number of watches from a Jewish-owned store in Arras and distributed them as gifts to their men. When Eicke discovered this, he simply reprimanded the men and had the watches collected and handed over to the Wehrmacht. This leniency was coupled with Eicke's explanation for his actions. He told the two officers and their men that the watches had to be returned not because they had been property of a Jewish shopkeeper, but because the army had previously laid claim to the shop and thus the SS men were technically guilty of stealing from their army colleagues.

Eicke also took a considerable interest in his men's sexual health. In an effort to relieve the boredom of occupation duties in France, Eicke ensured several brothels in Bordeaux be available solely for the use of *Totenkopf* soldiers. He complemented this with the implementation of strict sanitary regulations and warned his troops that he would consider the catching of venereal disease a racial crime and would court-martial any SS man who contracted gonorrhoea. Eicke ordered all officers and men to report to their medical officers for periodic check-ups to see if they had caught such infections. He then secretly told the doctors to send him the names of any men with venereal disease so that they could be punished. Almost all of *Totenkopf's* doctors ignored the order and did not return the names of those men they were treating in order to save them from prosecution.

clear once the French campaign had finished and the division had some time to deal with the disciplinary cases that had arisen during the fighting. Furthermore, a large number of reservists had been drafted into the division and these men were not so well disciplined as the *Totenkopf* veterans. Between June and November 1940, the division's court martial system dealt with 137 cases. Most involved such things as traffic accidents, but 37 involved criminal activities. The majority was cases such as robbery, rape or insubordination, all of which were punishable by expulsion from the SS and imprisonment. Eicke usually changed this prison sentence to an indefinite term of forced labour in the engineer battalion. Even so, this was not really a large number of criminal cases. This was largely because most of the more serious criminal charges involved acts against French civilians or their

The rest of the *Waffen-SS* took great delight in the stupidity of Eicke's gonorrhoea order and, in December 1940, the story reached Himmler. The prim *SS-Reichsführer* was livid and, in a telling indicator of Himmler's morality and sense of priority, Eicke received the most serious reprimand of his SS career. Himmler told the *Totenkopf* commander that he was violating basic German civil laws and bluntly claimed he was disgusted by Eicke's pettiness. Himmler continued by telling Eicke that he had embarrassed the entire SS with these crazy instructions and left Himmler doubtful of Eicke's mental health and fitness to command. Himmler ended by

Below: Rifle training at Bad Tölz. Before 1939, cadets would be sent to a platoon leader's course at Dachau after completing the officer candidate course. After 1939, cadets would be sent to a weapons training school.

ordering Eicke to cease punishing those soldiers with venereal disease.

After the French campaign, *Totenkopf* was committed to the invasion of the Soviet Union. From then onwards – apart from four months in France in late 1942 to early 1943 rebuilding after the loss of most of the division in the Demyansk pocket and occasional periods in reserve – *Totenkopf* saw almost constant action. Under these circumstances, the division seems to have few, if any, disciplinary or morale problems. All troops can get restless when they have little to do; Eicke's response was always a harsh training and disciplinary regime. The success of his approach is demonstrated by *Totenkopf*'s endurance and its formidable combat record. Eicke may have been rigid, narrow-minded and positively brutal when it came to the enforcement of standards of behaviour, but, from a military point of view, it seems to have worked.

Given the variety of uniforms issued, the exigencies of the Russia winter and the propensity of SS men, particularly officers, to customise their uniforms and ignore uniform regulations, this survey can give little more than a generalised account of the clothing issued to the *Waffen-SS* in general and *Totenkopf* in particular. It also concentrates largely on combat uniforms rather than walking-out dress, fatigues, PT kit and the like. (For those interested in this aspect of the *Waffen-SS*, there are far more detailed and authoritative accounts available.)

INSIGNIA

The *SS-Reichsführer* Heinrich Himmler was fascinated by Teutonic and Nordic mythology and this obsession shaped the insignia of the *Waffen-SS* and, by extension, *Totenkopf*. The double Sig rune 'lightning flash' denoting the SS was, probably, the most famous and commonly recognised piece of SS insignia. Close behind, perhaps, was the symbol of the pre-war concentration camp guards and later the division created from these formations. This was, of course, the *Totenkopf* or 'death's head', the origins and symbolism of which have already been discussed in the first chapter. It was an extremely potent piece of imagery and, despite being the only symbol common to all branches of the SS, it was worn with considerable pride by Eicke and his division as their symbol from 29 March 1936. Eicke had, in fact, been referring to himself as the *Führer der Totenkopfverbände* (Leader/Commander of the Death's Head Units) since December of the previous year.

The *Totenkopf* division used standard SS rank insignia and coloured *Waffenfarben* on the tunic shoulder straps and cap piping to denote the soldier's branch of service. Traditionally, in the pre-war SS, rank patches had been displayed on the left collar. Army pattern shoulder straps were introduced to the SS-VT, *Leibstandarte* and *Totenkopfverbände* in March 1938. Thus, *Waffen-SS* men would have their rank displayed twice. On the left collar patch was their SS rank; on the shoulder straps was the army equivalent. This duplication was clearly unnecessary. Himmler, however, determined to maintain the distinctiveness

of the *Waffen-SS*, decreed that SS ranks should still be displayed. This caused all sorts of problems when the armed SS went to war with the *Wehrmacht* in September 1939. Ordinary German soldiers were confused by the SS rank system and did not know whether they were supposed to salute the SS soldier or were obliged to obey his orders. It thus became obvious that *Waffen-SS* rank badges should correspond to those of the armed forces and, when the first *Waffen-SS* field divisions were formed in October 1939, their personnel no longer wore SS rank patches. Instead, on their collars, the men from *Verfügungstruppe*, the *Polizei* Division and the expanded *Leibstandarte* regiment received matching collar patches with either the double Sig rune or death's head symbol on either side. *Totenkopf* was an exception, as its men had always worn a death's head badge.

All *Waffen-SS* men, in theory, now had their ranks depicted solely on their shoulder straps, as was the case in the German Army. However, in contravention of this, many pre-war, non-*Totenkopf Waffen-SS* officers and men continued to wear their SS rank patches. Himmler's order, however, soon had to be rescinded. The increased use of camouflaged smocks within the SS caused problems. These smocks covered the shoulder straps and all insignia apart from collar patches. Thus, Hitler was forced on 10 May 1940 to reintroduce the SS rank patch for all *Waffen-SS* members. Contrary to this order, many *Totenkopf* troops continued to wear their traditional double collar patch well into 1941. From then on, the basic SS rune collar patch became standard for all German and Germanic *Waffen-SS* formations except *Totenkopf* units, whose men still wore the death's head throughout the conflict.

Cuff titles, which were woven black tapes worn on the lower left sleeve of the tunic and greatcoat, were a distinctive part of SS uniform and, quite apart from identifying the unit of the wearer, were responsible to some extent for adding to the esprit de corps. All of the pre-war *Totenkopfverbände* regiments – *Oberbayern*, *Brandenburg*, *Thüringen*, *Ostmark*, *Dietrich Eckart* and *Heimwehr Danzig* – had their own cuff title embroidered in Gothic lettering. Divisional cuff titles were

Above: These *Totenkopfverbände* **men on a training exercise before the war are wearing the standard** *Wehrmacht* **greatcoat and M1934** *Feldmützen* **(forage caps). By 1942, winter clothing had become more sophisticated.**

introduced in 1942 and worn by divisional personnel who were not entitled to regimental cuff titles. The later *Totenkopf* grenadier regiments *Thule* (1942) and *Theodor Eicke* also had their own cuff titles.

THE SS EAGLE

The SS arm eagle was also a distinctive part of the *Waffen-SS* uniform. Only the army, navy and air force wore the eagle on their right breast, thus the armed SS wore theirs on the upper left arm. The pattern, introduced in 1936, was a right-facing eagle with dipping wings. This was discontinued in 1938, although it continued to be worn by some veterans until 1943. The definitive SS eagle was introduced in 1938, with a left-facing eagle and straight wings tapering to a point. There were minor variations; the eagle from 1938–41 had a pronounced square head, its successor from 1942–43 had a less pronounced curved head and the final version had a shallow round head. The eagle was usually depicted in white or silver grey cotton thread on black. *Waffen-SS* men also wore

trade badges to identify their special skills. These badges in the shape of black cloth diamonds were worn on the lower left sleeve above the cuff title. Each badge was awarded on the successful completion of an SS training course; however, those who completed army courses had to wear the relevant army badge.

In the early years of Nazi rule, members of the SS concentration camp guard formations were issued with the 1934 *Reichszeugmeisterai der NSDAP* (RZM – Nazi Party Contracts Office) steel helmet. It was lighter than the standard army helmet, as the armed SS's role at that time was restricted to internal security duties. The RZM helmet was popular and remained in service until 1939. Once the *Waffen-SS* went to war, the lightweight helmet was replaced by the standard army M 1935 *Stahlhelm*. In March 1935, however, the concentration guard units were authorised to display a silver death's head emblem on the left side of their

Above: Members of the *Totenkopfverbände* on exercise with a field piece shortly before the outbreak of war in September 1939. At this stage the *Waffen-SS* were still using standard *Wehrmacht* uniforms.

helmets. This distinguished them from the *Leibstandarte*, who at the time wore a shield in the national colours (red, white and black), and the SS-VT, who wore a white-bordered black swastika, both also on the left side of their helmets. All units had the SS runes on the right. This insignia was only briefly in use, however, as SS helmet insignia was standardised in August 1935. From then on, all SS helmets had black SS runes in a white shield on the right side of the helmet and a red shield bearing a white disc with a black swastika on the left. In March 1940, the black, white and red swastika insignia on the left of the helmet was removed for camouflage reasons. The helmets were also painted darker shades of field grey and given a rougher texture that did not reflect the light. In 1942, the design of the helmet changed. The smooth inward crimping of the helmet was removed for economic reasons and, in November 1943, the SS runes on the right side of the helmet were removed.

FIELD CAPS

In March 1936, the other ranks' ship-shaped field caps, known as *schiffchen*, were manufactured in black to wear with the black service walking-out uniform. *Totenkopfverbände* wore earth-brown field caps while on duty in the concentration camps. When field grey

Below: By the time of the invasion of France in 1940, the *Totenkopf* Division had re-equipped with the famous *Waffen-SS* 'tiger jacket' camouflaged smock and helmet cover. The machine gun is a Czech-designed MG (30)t.

combat uniforms were distributed to the armed SS in 1937, this headgear was replaced with a field grey version. Officers who wore peaked caps known as *schrimmütze* now had caps with a field grey top. In February 1938, a new cap was introduced for NCOs. It was similar to the *schrimmütze*, but the peak was made of cloth and there was no stiffener in the crown. It could be folded easily and put in a pocket or backpack, and was thus nicknamed the 'crusher'. Many NCOs who later became officers continued to wear these caps throughout the war (some accounts claim that such caps were issued to both officers and NCOs). It was only in December 1938 that a field cap was specifically authorised for *Waffen-SS* officers. Its insignia consisted of the SS eagle and the *Totenkopf* badge. In October 1940, the other ranks' field cap was replaced by a new style identical to the officers' version and featuring a machine-woven eagle and

Right: Soldiers of the *Totenkopf* Division at Kursk in 1943. The standard *Waffen-SS* uniforms and webbing are clear to see, as is the *Totenkopf* (or death's head) collar patch identifying members of the division within the *Waffen-SS*.

death's head, rather than metal buttons. The *Einheitsfeldmütze Modell 1943* began to replace the *schiffchen* field cap in 1943. It was based on the mountain and tropical field caps, but had a slightly longer peak than the mountain cap. The flap fastened at the front with two buttons, although this was later reduced to one. The usual insignia was a woven death's head on the front of the crown with an eagle on the left of the flap. An officers' version had silver crown piping.

TUNICS

The first armed SS units wore 1932 pattern black uniform on all occasions. It was identical to the uniform worn by the *Allgemeine-SS*. Although impressive in appearance, it was somewhat impractical in the barracks or in the field. Thus, a lightweight grey-white cotton drill uniform was issued in the summer of 1933. In March 1936, a brown uniform was produced for the everyday duties of the *SS-Totenkopfverbände* working within the camps. The black uniform remained in use by the sentries on the main gates, who were visible to the public. This uniform was replaced for the camp guards with a new standard field grey uniform that was also issued to the SS-VT and *Leibstandarte*. This tunic was based on the army *feldbluse* (tunic), although it had slanting slash side pockets and a black-and-silver piped collar.

However, the expansion of the *Waffen-SS* at the end of 1939 and the formation of the new SS divisions, including *Totenkopf*, meant that there were not enough special SS tunics to go around. Army-issue tunics were therefore distributed to the new SS divisions. Himmler was keen that the SS retain its distinctive style. In the winter of 1939–40, he issued a series of complicated and often contradictory orders as to whom should wear what type of uniform and whether those uniforms should be buttoned or unbuttoned to the neck and similar trivial criteria. These orders were generally ignored by *Waffen-SS*

troops and a considerable mixture of dress was worn by all ranks.

From the French campaign onwards, however, the wearing of standard army tunics became universal throughout the *Waffen-SS*. This remained the case throughout the war, although, for reasons of economy, the tunics were altered for both the *Waffen-SS* and the army. In 1942, pockets were made without pleats in an effort to save cloth and, in 1943, the lower edges

of the pocket flaps were straightened. Also, the 1943 tunic contained a drastic reduction in the percentage of wool in the garment, with the ensuing effects of lower tensile strength and poorer thermal qualities.

In September 1944, an entirely new form of service dress tunic was issued for all German ground combat units based on British army battle dress. In theory, it standardised the variations in field grey that had been seen in various military and paramilitary formations. In practice, numerous variations in colour occurred. This uniform required considerably less cloth than its predecessors. It was extremely unpopular, but was never issued in great enough quantities to change the appearance of *Totenkopf* units drastically. Officers' tunics from December 1939 onwards were according to regulations the same as those for enlisted men. Officers would therefore either wear basic issue tunics or privately tailored

blouses, depending on their means or their desire to be distinctive.

In accordance with the issuing of the 1937 patterned tunic, new straight-leg pattern SS field trousers or feldhose for wearing with jackboots were introduced. In July 1942, wedge trousers, or keilhose, which tapered to fit inside the newly issued ankle boots and gaiters (replacing the infamous jackboot to save precious leather), entered service. Officers very often wore riding breeches while in the field. These were usually reinforced on the inner leg and seat. In August 1944, officers were ordered to wear straight trousers of the other patterns to ensure uniformity. This order was rarely obeyed, as numerous photographs of SS units prove.

Above: Winter clothing as modelled by members of *Totenkopf* **launching a counter-attack during the fighting in the Demyansk pocket in early 1942. Note the corrugated gas mask holders, by now normally used for storage.**

Camouflage

The most innovative *Waffen-SS* contribution to military uniform was the use of standardised camouflage. This has had a profound effect on military uniform and, as a result, almost all modern soldiers now wear camouflage clothing when in the field. In February 1937, Wilhelm Brandt, an *SS-Sturmbannführer* and commander of the SS-VT reconnaissance battalion, in conjunction with a Munich professor, Johan Georg Otto Schick, began work on designs for camouflaged

Right: A *Totenkopf* SS-*Hauptsturmführer* stands in front of a captured Soviet T-34 which has had the division's death's head symbol painted on the front of the turret to avoid attracting 'friendly fire' from other units.

clothing for SS troops. Their prototype groundsheets and helmet covers were tested by the SS-VT regiment *Deutschland* the following December. The exercise convinced the armed SS that use of camouflaged clothing would reduce casualties by 15 per cent. The SS was granted patents so that the design could not be copied by the army and, in November 1938, production began. Although there were problems in getting hold of enough waterproof cotton duck, 8400 groundsheets and 6800 helmet covers were supplied to the SS-VT. Smocks were also produced.

Camouflaged clothing did not see widespread service in the Polish campaign, but it received high praise and wide-scale production of camouflaged smocks for all field units of the *Waffen-SS* began in the summer of 1940. Most *Waffen-SS* combat troops, however, were issued the famous SS tiger jacket camouflaged smock for use in the invasion of France. These were made of waterproof cotton duck and were reversible. Different shades of camouflage were printed on the two sides. One was predominantly green for the spring and summer, and the other brown for autumn and winter. The patterns varied widely, but a combination of leaf shapes and spots were characteristic. The smocks had elasticated waists and cuffs. The cuff's frills were often tucked up the soldier's sleeve, under the cuff elastic. They had drawstring fastenings down the chest and vertical access slips for the pockets. Later smocks were often camouflaged only on one side and thus could not be reversed. Production of the smocks ceased in January 1944, but they continued to be worn until the end of the war.

In the smock's place, a new camouflage version of the field grey drill uniform was introduced in the same cut as the 1943 field uniform, in a spotted camouflage pattern on one side only. It could be worn over the standard field grey uniform in the winter. Insignia was limited to the eagle and swastika, and special rank badges on the left sleeve. Distribution of

this uniform ceased between November 1944 and March 1945. The first item of camouflage to be widely issued to SS units, however, was the groundsheet. It was triangular, measuring 203cm x 203cm x 240cm (80in x 80in x 94in). It could be worn as a cape or poncho, or buttoned together with three others to make a four-man tent. By joining even more groundsheets, larger shelters could be built. In December 1943, the issue of groundsheets to men on the Eastern Front ceased for economic reasons and, in September 1944, production ceased entirely. The steel helmet cover was produced from the same material and attached to the helmet by three clips. Covers made from 1942 onwards had loops sewn on to hold foliage for additional camouflage effect.

For *Totenkopf*'s armoured troops, a field grey *Panzerjacke*, or tank tunic, was issued from August

1942 onwards. This was a short, tight-fitting, double-breasted black jacket which fastened with concealed buttons. However, in January 1943, all SS panzer crews received a one-piece camouflaged combination work uniform made out of waterproof cotton duck. This was widely used during the battle of Kharkov, but proved very unpopular because of the difficulty of getting in and out of it. This uniform was discontinued in January 1944 and a lightweight panzer uniform in camouflage drill was introduced and saw widespread service.

A double-breasted greatcoat or mantle in a similar pattern to that of the army was issued to SS-VT and SS-*Totenkopfverbände* which was given a dark green collar to distinguish it as an SS uniform. As the war progressed and the quality of these coats declined, officers often had their coats tailor-made. Thus, a wide variety of greatcoat styles saw service with the SS. Officers were also allowed to purchase leather greatcoats in field grey, but few junior officers did so because of their great expense. Many simply bought the 1938 field grey raincoat made of rubberised cotton twill. Others used the regulation motorcyclist's coat. The disastrous 1941–42 winter campaign showed the inadequacy of German cold-weather clothing. The standard greatcoat had proved utterly inadequate. Various fur, sheepskin and woollen, waistcoats, caps and coats were issued as an expedient short-term measure. Snow coats intended for mountain troops serving in Norway were diverted to the East, as were civilian items of clothing collected in Germany. Captured Soviet winter clothing was often used as well. In 1942, the *Waffen-SS* developed its own winter combat uniform consisting of a heavy fur-lined parka in grey waterproof gabardine. Undyed woollen hooded smocks and trousers were also issued when snow lay on the ground. In the winter of 1943–44, the *Waffen-SS* winter uniform that would see service until the end of the war was issued. It comprised of hood,

Left: A *Totenkopf* soldier during the fighting for the Demyansk pocket in early 1942. On the whole, the men of the *Waffen-SS* were better equipped for the first winter in the Soviet Union than their *Wehrmacht* counterparts.

jacket, trousers and mittens made of two layers of windproof material, with a wool rayon interlining. The outfit was reversible, being white on one side and brown autumn camouflage on the other, and could be worn over the normal field uniform.

BOOTS

The standard footwear of the first SS troops consisted of two pairs of jackboots. Officers often wore high, black riding boots which had been privately purchased. From July 1942 onwards, a standard lace-up ankle boot was issued to most *Waffen-SS* troops instead of the jackboot. Short boots and gaiters proved very unpopular with most SS and army troops, who often referred to them as 'retreat gaiters' and hung on to their jackboots as long as possible despite the fact that these were prone to cause varicose veins in later life. As the quality of German boots declined during the war, *Waffen-SS* troops often took to wearing captured enemy boots. In the appalling cold of the Russian winter, Soviet felt boots (valenki) which gave excellent protection from the extremes of the weather, were particularly popular if they could be removed from their previous owners before they were frozen onto the corpse – although German troops were not averse to resorting fairly grisly methods of removal. The popular steel-shod jackboots, while fine in more temperate weather, proved utterly inadequate in the winter and tended to hasten the process of frostbite. In the case of boots at least, there was no difference between the SS and the army.

The most common webbing arrangement was based around a black leather waist belt with a 1931 pattern SS box buckle of nickel-plated steel or matt grey alloy. The belt was issued to all NCOs and enlisted men, and worn with all orders of dress. The officer's belt was circular and somewhat flimsy, but Himmler refused to modify its design because 'it had been designed by the Führer himself and based on his sketches'. Thus SS officers had to either endure the belt buckle coming undone or breaking at inopportune moments, or adopt the standard enlisted man's belt or the two-pronged open-faced army buckle. Added to this basic webbing, an SS man typically wore

Right: The *Waffen-SS* **introduced the camouflage smock after extensive tests which demonstrated its effectiveness in combat. Here a machine gun team in the Soviet Union are firing the excellent 7.92mm MG34.**

the 1939 *Gefechtsgepäck*, which was a webbing leather, A-frame assault harness clipped to D-rings behind each shoulder brace, supported by straps and buckles, mess-tins, bag of tent pegs, and sometimes an 'iron ration' bag. When in full marching order, a pack was carried to which the greatcoat and groundsheet could be clipped. The pack would be left with the unit transport, however, when combat was imminent. The gas mask was slung separately. The soldier's bread bag, which also contained any small personal kit, a field cap and rations, hung on the right. The water canteen was usually clipped to the bag. The entrenching tool – the most common being the 1938 model – was suspended on the left.

AMMUNITION POUCHES

Most riflemen wore a bayonet frog and the model 1911 cartridge pouches. Each pouch had three individually fastened pockets. A front line infantryman would wear two, which carried a total of 60 rounds. Troops armed with machine pistols carried one or two special belt pouches which each held three magazines. These were initially made of leather, although canvas pouches were later introduced. Virtually all leather parts of webbing equipment were later replaced with canvas or other, synthetic materials. Later in the war, when the *Sturmgewehr 44* assault rifle began to see service, new large, curved ammunition pouches which held three magazines were issued. Pistol holsters were usually issued with the weapon and often carried a spare magazine and possibly cleaning accoutrements. As with most German belt kit and webbing furniture, leather holsters were gradually replaced by canvas equivalents as the war progressed. Holsters were carried on the belt on the left side, with the pistol butt facing forward while on operations. As with all items of uniform, there was a great deal of variation and personal adaptation of webbing equipment.

CHAPTER THREE

BLOODING

After the extensive preparation and training, when the *Totenkopfverbände* went to war in 1939, it was an anticlimax. However, within the year they were part of the new *Totenkopf* Division, which would begin to forge its fearsome reputation in the invasion of France.

The first German campaign of World War II was crucial in the shaping of the *Totenkopfverbände* and preparing the unit for conversion to full divisional status. Charles Sydnor eloquently described the campaign's importance for *Totenkopf* in his book *Soldiers of Destruction*: 'In the harsh crucible of Poland, the grim heritage of the concentration camps was violently transformed into an ethos of war that became and remained a key element in the *Waffen-SS* character of Eicke's *Totenkopf* formations.' *Totenkopf* did not play any role in the German campaign that destroyed the Polish armed forces; rather, it undertook a series of far less palatable (and less publicised) activities behind German lines.

THE POLISH CAMPAIGN

At 0445 hours on 1 September 1939, five German armies invaded Poland from the north, west and south, supported by the *Luftwaffe*, which dominated the skies. The Germans thrust two pincers deep into Poland towards Warsaw, while subsidiary drives spanned out from the main axes of advance. The

Left: In the last weeks of peace, the *Gauleiter* of Danzig presents *SS-Obersturmbannführer* Götze of *SS Heimwehr-Danzig* (later part of the *Totenkopf* Division) with a banner during a parade in response to Polish 'warmongering'.

Poles fought with great courage, but the German advance, spearheaded by the German Army's panzer divisions, brushed aside Polish resistance and proved the effectiveness of Heinz Guderian's theories of armoured warfare, soon dubbed by the Western press as *blitzkrieg*. Poland fell in 18 days. It was an astounding military victory, but *Totenkopf* did not contribute towards it.

On 7 September 1939, six days into the campaign, Himmler designated the three *Totenkopfverbände* regiments *Oberbayern*, *Thüringen* and *Brandenburg* – which had moved from their depots into Upper Silesia near the Polish border – as *Einsatzgruppen* (action groups) under Eicke's command. *Oberbayern* and *Thüringen* were sent into the 10th Army's area of operation and were located between Upper Silesia and the Vistula south of Warsaw. *Brandenburg* followed the 8th Army through Poznan and west central Poland. Eicke had been appointed *Höhere SS Polizei Führer* for the areas of Poland captured by the 10th and 8th Armies by Himmler and was responsible for 'pacifying' the local population. Unsurprisingly, given the background of Eicke and his Death's Head Units, the methods that he used were extremely brutal.

In fact, they were the perfect tool to implement the fate that Hitler intended for considerable elements of Polish society. He declared in a speech to his services

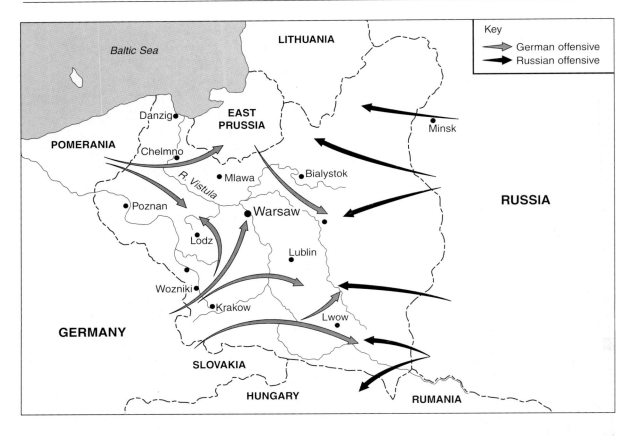

chiefs, on 22 August 1939, that he intended to liqui-date the Polish leadership and intelligentsia. This was all part of Hitler's plan to produce 'a leaderless labour force' to serve Germany. Liquidate was exactly what the *Totenkopfverbände einsatzgruppen* did. They did not simply limit themselves to the 'liq-uidation' of the Polish leadership, but extended such treatment to other groups that did not fit into the Nazi canon.

GERMAN ATROCITIES

Like so much of the Nazi and SS system (for this period of the war, at least), the *Totenkopf* regiments kept scrupulous records, which makes detailing their activities comparatively simple. *Brandenburg*, com-manded by *Standartenführer* Paul Nostitz, entered Poland on 13 September and at once went into action, arresting and shooting large numbers of 'sus-

Above: Although Eicke had high hopes that his units would be used in action during the invasion of Poland, most of the *Totenkopfverbände* were used for *Einsatz-gruppen* activities against Poles behind the front lines.

Above right: Troops of *SS Totenkopfstandarte Heimwehr Danzig* prepare to attack the Danzig post office in the opening hours of the Polish campaign. However, most of the *Totenkopfstandarte* were not used in combat in 1939.

picious elements, plunderers, insurgents, Jews and Poles'. A typically savage action undertaken by *Brandenburg* was the four-day 'Jewish action' under-taken against Wloclawek northwest of Warsaw between 22 and 26 September 1939. Synagogues were burnt, Jewish businesses looted and leading members of the Jewish community rounded up and executed. In the midst of these atrocities, Eicke ordered Nostitz

to detach two battalions to Bydgoszcz, to deal with the 'intelligentsia' in the area. Following a death list of intellectuals and political leaders drawn up by the Security Police, these two battalions killed some 800 Poles in the area over the subsequent two days.

The other *Totenkopfverbände* regiments sent into Poland carried out similar activities across Poland. *Heimwehr Danzig* – which later formed the nucleus of *Totenkopf*'s artillery battalion when it became a division – shot a number of Polish civilians while in Pomerania. *Oberbayern* and *Thüringen*, operating in the rear area of the 10th Army, carried out a number of mass shootings of political leaders, clergy, teachers, Jews and Polish soldiers in south central Poland.

When the original *Totenkopf standarten* left Poland in late October 1939, they were replaced by the new *Totenkopfverbände*, including the 12th *Standarte*, which followed *Brandenburg* into Pomerania and behaved similarly. It was here that one company killed more than a thousand helpless mental hospital patients at Owinsk. The 12th *Standarte* later provided combat replacements for the division in autumn 1941. Due to the efforts of formations such as the *Totenkopf* regiments in Poland, by 27 September, Reinhard Heydrich could record that he reckoned only three per cent of Polish upper classes had survived the massacres, which had claimed at least 10,000 civilians that September and October.

A number of senior army personnel were extremely perturbed at what had taken place behind the German advance. Lieutenant General Alfred Boehm-Tettelbach, who commanded the German Army rear area in which Wloclawek lay, was horrified by *Brandenburg*'s behaviour. Quite apart from the unit's sheer brutality, Boehm-Tettelbach was angered when Nostitz repeatedly refused to undertake standard security operations such as combing the woods south of Wloclawek for stragglers from the fighting. It seemed to the general that the SS were much happier staying in the town and beating up and murdering Jews and Polish civilians. It was clear to him that the SS were there purely for this reason. This was further

confirmed by *SS-Gruppenführer* Günther Pancke from Eicke's headquarters, who told Boehm-Tettelbach that the SS were not under army control. The soldier concluded – correctly enough – that *Brandenburg* was in the area solely to terrorise the local Jews.

Boehm-Tettelbach sent his report on *Brandenburg*'s actions to the commander of the 8th Army, Colonel General Blaskowitz. He was equally appalled and compiled a long list of the *Totenkopfverbände*'s crimes and sent it to the Commander-in-Chief of the German Army (*Wehrmacht*), Walther von Brauchitsch. General Blaskowitz was disgusted by their bestial treatment of the Poles and the manner in which the executions took place. Neither was he very impressed

Left: Jews murdered by Eicke's *Totenkopfstandarte Brandenburg* in Poland during their activities as *Einsatzgruppen*. The unit committed a string of atrocities against Polish Jews and intellectuals near Wloclawek.

by the public drunkenness and looting undertaken by some of the more recently formed *Totenkopf* units. Brauchitsch met Himmler to discuss the report and the *SS-Reichsführer* admitted that 'mistakes had been made in the implementation of "ethnic policy" in Poland'. He promised that in future such tasks would be carried out 'in as considerate manner as possible and with a minimum of bloodshed'. Himmler also told Brauchitsch that the SS wanted good relations with the army and that it was not his intention to 'establish an army alongside the army'. All of which was untrue. The Commander-in-Chief, however, took the issue no further.

Even if he had had the courage to pursue the issue, he would not have met with much success. This was amply illustrated by Hitler's response to army complaints of SS atrocities in Poland. The Führer said that the generals 'should not interfere in such matters but restrict themselves to their military duties'. Indeed, on the rare occasions the army authorities attempted to prosecute SS personnel, Himmler invariably managed to have the charges dropped or sentences commuted. He also persuaded Hitler to remove the *Waffen-SS* from the jurisdiction of military courts in wartime, which the Führer did on 17 October 1939. This freed the SS from the *Wehrmacht*'s legal jurisdiction. Although the SS were, in theory, still subject to the military code, it was now administered by special SS courts.

THE *WAFFEN-SS* DIVISIONS

Himmler successfully weathered army complaints about the SS's behaviour in Poland and also managed to remove the SS from army legal control. He now turned to another, even more important victory: the creation of full *Waffen-SS* (as the armed SS had officially become) divisions, and a large-scale expansion of SS personnel. The SS regiments that had seen combat in Poland had suffered heavy casualties. The army

used this as argument to demand that the armed formations should be disbanded. Himmler claimed that the casualties were due to the SS units having to serve under unfamiliar commanders and thus the SS should be able to form its own divisions under SS commanders. In the first week of October, Hitler agreed to the formation of three SS divisions.

Himmler used the three regiments of the SS-VT to form the *SS-Verfügungs* Division and expanded *Leibstandarte* to the size of a reinforced regiment. This exhausted his battle-experienced troops. If the other divisions were constructed of raw recruits, it would take at least six months to train them to an adequate standard, time he could ill afford if they were to be ready for the campaign that Hitler intended to launch in the West. Himmler therefore decided to draw on the paramilitary-trained units at his disposal. So, for the second of three divisions, he turned to Eicke's *Totenkopfverbände*. The final division, *Polizei*, was drawn from the *Ordungspolizei*. The formation of these latter two divisions also allowed Himmler to undertake a large-scale expansion of the SS in order to replace the *Totenkopfverbände* and *Ordungspolizei* personnel used in the new *Waffen-SS* divisions.

Hitler gave his approval and, in one stroke, Himmler had broken the tight reign the Army High Command had held on the further development of the armed SS. It was a period of rapid expansion. As Himmler himself later recalled in a speech to senior SS officers in Posen on 4 October 1943, the expansion of the armed SS after the start of the war was 'fantastic' and carried out 'at absolutely terrific speed'. In 1939, the SS was only 'a few regiments, guard units, 8000 to 9000 strong – that is not even a division; all in all 25,000 to 28,000 men at the most'. Yet, within the year, its strength had reached 150,000 – a six-fold increase – and the *Waffen-SS* could begin to consider itself, as Himmler put it, 'the fourth branch of the *Wehrmacht*'.

Meanwhile, Eicke had returned from Poland to Dachau to organise the conversion of the *Totenkopfverbände* into the *Totenkopf* Division. *Totenkopf* had been designated as motorised and Eicke based the core of the formation around the three original

Totenkopf Standarten, which became motorised infantry regiments. *Heimwehr Danzig* formed the basis of the division's artillery regiment. *Totenkopf* also required a divisional staff, a signals battalion, an engineer battalion, a *Panzerjäger* or tank destroyer battalion, a reconnaissance battalion and support services such as supply, administration and pay, and postal battalions and medical and ambulance units. Such was the expansion that Eicke also had to draw on members of the SS-VT and police for extra manpower.

companies for each regiment. The artillery regiment was divided into three battalions: two light artillery, and one heavy. Each artillery battalion had three batteries, and each battery had four guns. The engineer battalion and tank destroyer battalion both had three companies and the reconnaissance battalion consisted of two motorcycle companies and an armoured car platoon. The signals battalion was divided into two; one company handled telephone communications, the other radios.

EICKE FORCED TO SCAVENGE

The most pressing problem facing Eicke and his staff was the combat and technical training of the troops – although he also faced difficulties procuring the necessary weapons and equipment for a motorised division. By the third week of October, all the men assigned to the division had arrived at Dachau and Eicke at once began a rigorous training programme for his men. There were lectures, exercises and weapons training programmes and, in November, as the men became more capable, the exercises broadened in scale from platoon to company, battalion and, finally, regimental level. The officers were also trained extensively in the problems of command. By late November, Eicke began taking the entire division on practice marches so that the men could become familiar with moving and assembling large-scale motorised units. As the *Wehrmacht* accepted the inevitable, it began to take men from *Totenkopf* on its specialist training courses. The main problem remained lack of weaponry, which hampered the division's training schedule. Eicke scavenged weapons and vehicles from across Germany. He begged, borrowed and stole pretty much everything the division needed, apart from artillery. He also worked hard to introduce the same spirit of esprit de corps and high level of morale that had been evident in the pre-war *Totenkopfverbände*, while struggling to ensure his men

Eicke based *Totenkopf* on traditional army lines, although admittedly he had three motorised infantry regiments to the German Army's two. The infantry regiments were divided into three battalions, or four companies each. There were also two replacement

did not enjoy the dubious pleasures of nearby Munich too much.

In the midst of this, in early December, *Totenkopf* was ordered to move to Ludwigsberg, just north of Stuttgart, and placed in the second-line reserve for the forthcoming attack on the West. Although the move disrupted Eicke's training programme, it did allow him and his staff to plan the division's dispositions in battle. Adapting slightly the army regulations for this, Eicke felt, in common with many SS commanders, that the army's doctrine of offensive speed could be improved by the concentration of as much forward firepower as possible and the reckless aggressive pursuit of the attack. Thus, he placed a heavier weight of infantry, artillery and reconnaissance vehicles in the van of the division. Eicke had no high-level military training, nor had he much interest in military theory. His basic belief – characterised by the performance of *Totenkopf* in the offensive – was that all possible means should be used to batter through the enemy line as aggressively as possible. Meanwhile, he continued to hector SS and army authorities for equipment, weapons and vehicles.

Eicke's despair at the gaps in *Totenkopf*'s inventory was matched by his operations officer, *SS-Standartenführer* Cassius Freiherr von Montigny, who was one of the few senior officers in *Totenkopf* without a background in the concentration camp system. Montigny was alarmed by the weaknesses shown in recent exercises. Regimental commanders lacked skill in handling large motorised formations; the division lacked adequately skilled mechanics and was prone to producing huge traffic jams when on the move. Furthermore, the division's coordination of firepower was lacking and, perhaps most seriously, he concluded that leadership was poor amongst officers and discipline sorely lacking as well. Montigny put his considerable talents into rectifying these problems in the months before the opening of the French campaign. It is a testament to his skills that *Totenkopf* performed as well as it did.

In February, the Army High Command finally assigned *Totenkopf* its role in the forthcoming Western campaign. Eicke had hoped that *Totenkopf* would be

Right: A *Totenkopf* anti-tank gun, a 3.7cm Pak 35/36, seen on 20 May 1940 with its crew. The following day they would discover its ineffectiveness against the heavy Matilda tanks of the British outside Arras.

in the vanguard of the assault. However, it was assigned to the 2nd Army, an untrained reserve composed of freshly formed infantry divisions and *Totenkopf*. Both Eicke and Himmler complained, but the army command refused to reassign the division. As the weather improved, however, Eicke and Montigny were able to increase and intensify the training programme. By April, such progress had been made that Eicke was able to give a full-scale warfighting demonstration by *Totenkopf*'s Infantry Regiment No. 1 to the commander of the 2nd Army, Colonel General von Weichs. The general was mightily impressed and promised to do something about Eicke's long-running quest for heavy guns for his artillery battalion. Soon enough he provided enough 150-mm guns for one battery. On 19 April, all leave was cancelled and security measures tightened. Anticipation in the division heightened. On 9 May 1940, the 2nd Army signalled Eicke to have *Totenkopf* Division on full alert by dawn the following morning and ready to move at short notice. The campaign in France was about to begin.

THE BATTLE FOR FRANCE

Shortly after dawn on 10 May 1940, German tanks rolled across the Dutch and Belgian borders. Eicke distributed field rations to his units and told their commanders that they were to be ready to move within 12 hours. Meanwhile, as the battle for France opened, Eicke sat and nervously waited to discover the role that *Totenkopf* would play. He constantly telephoned 2nd Army headquarters, but they knew no more than he did. He probably reflected with some bitterness that the army, with some 157 divisions (only seven of which were motorised), had relegated *Totenkopf* to occupation duties, while the SS *Verfügung* Division and *Leibstandarte* had been committed to the first wave. Obviously, they believed that all Eicke (as a concentration camp commander) and his division

were capable of was mopping up after the fighting. After all, the Army Chief of Staff, General Halder, had noted that while the *Totenkopf* division presented a good appearance, they could not really be trusted with front line duty.

The German plan used three army groups that stretched the entire length of Germany's boundary with The Netherlands to Switzerland. Army Group B drove into The Netherlands and northern Belgium. In the centre, Army Group A, commanded by Colonel General Gerd von Rundstedt, delivered the crucial thrust through southern Belgium and north-eastern France. *Totenkopf* was included in the reserves available to Army Group A. Army Group C was positioned opposite the Maginot Line. Such was the success of the Army Group A offensive through the Ardennes that *Totenkopf*, as one of the few motorised formations available in the reserve, was soon released

to the main advance. Spearheaded by Heinz Guderian's 19th Panzer Corps, Rundstedt's forces drove hard to the Meuse, a key natural barrier. The first armoured unit to reach the river was General Erwin Rommel's 7th Panzer Division on 12 May. Rommel managed to get some men across the Meuse the following morning. By that evening, he had a pontoon bridge in place across the river. The 7th Panzer Division, followed quickly by the 5th Panzer Division, then drove westwards. However, it was Guderian who crossed the Meuse at Sedan, the key to cracking the French defensive line. Once Guderian had got his panzer corps across the river, the collapse of the French line was complete. The breakout carried his forces into the rear of the bulk of the British and French defenders in the north.

On 12 May, *Totenkopf* was ordered westwards to a staging area on the Belgian frontier. They waited here for another four days, however, before they were committed to the fray. On 14 May, as Army Group A prepared to break out from the Meuse, Eicke was alerted to stand by to move. Two more days passed while the Army Group A tanks drove spectacularly westwards, veered into the northern French plain and began the dash for the English Channel. The breakthrough had gone so quickly that German commanders were now desperate to call up reserves to plug the gaps caused by the rapidity of the German advance. Finally, on 17 May, *Totenkopf* was called out of reserve and assigned to Army Group A. Eicke was instructed to take his division across the southern Netherlands, through Belgium and into France to link up with General Hermann Hoth's 15th Panzer Corps, which included the 5th and 7th Panzer divisions. The division moved out just before dawn on 18 May. On their move through the Low Countries, *Totenkopf* encountered no enemy, as Army Group C had pushed the British and French back further west. Unsurprisingly, the division became snarled in the massive traffic jams to the rear of Army Group B.

First Casualties

On the morning of 19 May, Eicke received the division's orders. He was told to prepare for enemy counterattacks from the north and, shortly afterwards, ordered by 15th Panzer Corps to move into France towards the village of Le Cateaux, where Rommel's 7th Panzer Division was in serious difficulty in the face of a heavy French attack. Eicke sent *Totenkopf*'s 1st Infantry Regiment, commanded by *Standartenführer* Max Simon, with anti-tank engineer and artillery companies to relieve the pressure on Rommel. Thus, as Simon's regiment crossed the Sambre River and pushed towards Le Cateaux and Cambrai, they became the first *Totenkopf* troops to enter combat in a series of vicious house-to-house battles with French Moroccan troops in several small villages in their path. Once the Moroccans were dislodged, the French counterattacked with tanks, but the first infantry regiment held firm.

By mid-morning of 20 May, *Totenkopf* had cleared the areas to the north and east of Cambrai and taken

16,000 prisoners and a large haul of weapons and supplies, thus allowing Hoth's 15th Panzer Corps to resume its advance. *Totenkopf* had also taken its first wartime combat casualties, with 16 dead and 53 wounded, while claiming that they had killed some

*Below: *Totenkopf* soldiers take cover under artillery fire during their advance into France in 1940. British artillery fire would later hamper their move up to the perimeter around Dunkirk.*

200 Moroccan soldiers. It is testament to the ferocity of *Totenkopf*'s first day's fighting and quite possibly indicative of the racial attitudes of its troops that only 100 prisoners were Moroccan. As the division paused briefly, Eicke's supply column remained stuck in traffic in Belgium, so *Totenkopf* had to draw its rations from Rommel's 7th Panzer Division's stores.

While *Totenkopf* was entangled around Cambrai and Artois, and elements of the 7th Panzer Division reached Arras, the first German troops of the 2nd Panzer Division reached the English Channel. Here they cut off 40 French, British and Belgium divisions – nearly one million men – from the bulk of the French Army to the south. However, the Germans only occupied a thin 50–65-km (30–40-mile) wide strip. When the advance resumed, Eicke was ordered to join General Rudolf Schmidt's 39th Corps and advance westwards between the 8th Panzer Division to *Totenkopf*'s south and the 7th Panzer Division to the north. The intention of Army High Command

was to ensure that the cut-off Allied forces in the north did not re-establish contact with the French forces to the south. *Totenkopf* was part of the forces that would plug the gaps left by the rapidity of the German advance.

In fact, the British and French were indeed intending to cut through the extended German line and restore a common front. The only real hope that

Above: On 25/26 May Eicke told his division to attack across Le Bassée canal in contravention of Hitler's halt order. Here *Totenkopf* soldiers advance along a road supported by a captured Panhard armoured car.

the Allies had was to launch an effective blow against the flank and rear of the German spearhead. Lord Gort, the commander of the British Expeditionary

Force (BEF), began to organise a thrust southwards, exactly what the German commanders feared most. Given the horrendously disrupted state of Allied communications, this was not an easy task. Gort and Major General Harold Franklyn, from whose 5th Division the attacking force was drawn, assembled a mixture of disparate Anglo–French forces, a tank brigade, two territorial infantry battalions, some garrison troops and field artillery. A much-depleted French light mechanised division would support the attack from the west. The two French infantry divisions Gort was promised to support his eastern flank failed to materialise. Franklyn gave command of the attack to Major-General G. le Q. Martel, one of Britain's interwar tank pioneers. Martel had merely 58 Mark I and 16 Mark II 'Matilda' infantry tanks. The tanks were heavy, slow and cumbersome, and the Mark I was armed only with machine guns and the Mark II with a 2-pounder gun. This was of a similar calibre to the standard 37-mm German gun, but with considerably more hitting power. The French division could muster about 60 Somua tanks. Given the poor state of Allied intelligence and having been ordered to proceed without reconnaissance, Martel had no idea what German units faced him as he started to move south in two columns west of Arras at 1430 hours on 21 May 1940.

TOTENKOPF ATTACKED

In fact, he was about to come up against *Totenkopf.* By coincidence, the Germans had decided to move northwards and 7th Panzer, with *Totenkopf* to its west, rolled northwards directly into the path of Martel's counterattack. Very fortunately for *Totenkopf,* the brunt of the British attack in their area smashed right into the division's tank destroyer battalion. The battalion deployed quickly, but soon found that the unit's 37-mm Pak 35/36 anti-tank guns were utterly ineffective against the British Matildas' 60-mm armour. Rommel's 7th Panzer Division was having similar problems; one Matilda was discovered to have been hit 14 times by 37-mm shells before it was finally disabled. The British tanks rolled over two of *Totenkopf*'s anti-tank companies, causing considerable

casualties; the third company suffered particularly heavily. Those who stayed by their guns were killed at close range or even crushed by the 30-ton British tanks. Horrified by the ineffectiveness of their weapons, several companies fell backwards and at least one supply column left their vehicles and fled on the approach of British tanks. However, along with *Totenkopf*'s 3rd Infantry Regiment's heavy machine guns and mortars, they counterattacked again using grenades. They were repulsed with further heavy casualties. Eicke resorted to having the division's artillery fire on the British tanks over open sights before the arrival of Stuka Ju 87 dive-bombers finally blunted the assault.

Meanwhile, Rommel's division was hit by the main weight of Martel's attack and, according to Rommel's own account, verged on collapse and rout. Rommel drove from unit to unit, quickly organising a defence in depth and counterattacks, and used every available gun, artillery piece and *Luftwaffe* 88-mm anti-aircraft gun firing – similarly to Eicke's guns – over open sights, thus halting the British advance.

This account of *Totenkopf*'s role in stalling the British tanks varies with most versions of the battle. The emphasis has largely been on the rout of *Totenkopf*'s anti-tank companies and the embarrassment this caused the division. Much of this relies on Rommel's description of the battle, which heavily emphasised his own role in retrieving the situation. Even Heinz Guderian reckoned that the division 'showed signs of panic'. Yet the panic in Rommel's division was worse than that in *Totenkopf* and while obviously Rommel was instrumental in the battle – his division faced the bulk of the British attack – *Totenkopf* appears to have performed more creditably than is usually recognised.

Whatever the case, *Totenkopf* had sustained its worst casualties in its heaviest day's fighting so far. There were 39 dead, 66 wounded and two missing, mostly from the tank-destroyer battalion. The 7th Panzer Division fared considerably worse and the Germans lost some 20 tanks and a similar number of anti-tank guns. The British assault – although poorly organised and executed, launched without air cover or proper reconnaissance and utterly unsupported –

Above: Men of the *Totenkopf* Division manhandle a rubber dinghy down to the water. The British decision to fight along the line of the Le Bassée canal forced the unit to make a number of hazardous water crossings.

had given the Germans a real shock and the German advance paused temporarily. While Eicke's men rested, the SS general received fresh orders transferring the division to Erich Hoepner's 16th Panzer Corps, which already contained the 3rd and 4th Panzer Divisions and the *SS-Verfügungs* Division. Hoepner's corps was detailed with spearheading the attack on the British and French forces isolated in northern France and Belgium. Hoepner ordered Eicke to proceed northwards with caution, given what had happened at Arras. There was light contact on 22 May as *Totenkopf* resumed its advance, but this was easily brushed aside.

Hoepner ordered the division to move towards the town of Bethune, which lay astride La Bassée Canal, a natural defensive position that the British had retired behind. Eicke was then to reconnoitre the

area and find a suitable crossing point. He promptly disobeyed these orders and entered the town with the intention of crossing the canal. His men were forced to withdraw when they found the British strongly dug in in the town. As Eicke began to search for a crossing point, the British rapidly began to reinforce their positions on the opposite side of the canal. On the morning of 24 May, elements of the 3rd Infantry Regiment led personally by Eicke forced a crossing lower down the canal and established a bridgehead.

Just at this point, the division was ordered to break off the attack and withdraw back across the

Above: An unopposed river or canal crossing under way. This photograph clearly demonstrates how vulnerable the troops would be if they were to come under fire – as happened at the Le Bassée canal.

canal. This was due to Hitler's controversial halt order of 24 May, which held Army Group A's armour along the canal line and stopped all ground attacks. The purpose of this halt order was probably to preserve the tanks for the forthcoming battles in central France and allow the Luftwaffe the opportunity to attack the Allied troops in the pocket that had formed around the port of Dunkirk. Eicke was furious given the losses he had taken first in crossing the canal and then while withdrawing. Hoepner was equally angry when he found out that Eicke had disobeyed his orders, accusing the *Totenkopf* commander

of caring nothing for the lives of his men and allegedly calling Eicke 'a butcher' in front of his staff.

HALT ORDER CANCELLED

The halt order was rescinded on 26 May as the Army High Command realised that the British were preparing to make a stand along the canal line. In the meantime, *Totenkopf* had endured constant British shelling before Eicke finally received orders to attempt to cross the canal and establish a bridgehead. The 3rd Infantry Regiment commanded by *Standartenführer* Friedmann Götze managed to secure a foothold on the other side that night. The 2nd Infantry Regiment under Heinz Bertling also managed to get across, but against much stiffer resistance. Behind them, the engineers hastily erected pontoon bridges across the canal.

Hoepner then ordered Eicke to begin a general advance across the canal and to take Bethume. The Germans did not, however, know how well the British troops of the 2nd Division had dug in in front of them, nor did they know that the defenders were determined to buy time for the troops behind them who were being evacuated from Dunkirk. Thus the *Totenkopf* troops became involved in their most desperate and bitter fighting of the entire campaign.

FIRST CASUALTIES

The offensive resumed on 27 May. Götze's 3rd Infantry Regiment, supported by tanks of the 4th Panzer Division, advanced quickly and overwhelmed the British defenders around Locon, before pausing

for the rest of the division to catch up. However, to the north, Bertling's 2nd Infantry Regiment soon hit problems. Faced with the task of taking Bethune, held by the 1st battalion of the 8th Lancashire Fusiliers, the 2nd Regiment was sucked into desperate house-to-house, hand-to-hand fighting against the determined British defenders. Bertling had overextended himself and was soon getting the worst of the fighting. British counterattacks broke up his advance and began to reduce the pockets that the regiment still held in the village.

Bertling lost radio contact with the divisional HQ, but it was obvious to Eicke that the 2nd Infantry Regiment was in serious trouble and he detached one of Götze's battalions to dislodge the British in the vicinity of Le Cornet Malo and La Paradis. Götze decided to lead the battalion personally and was killed almost immediately (by a sniper), as the battalion made its way northwards. This came on top of the incapacitation of Montigny, the division's operations officer and one of its more able soldiers, who had collapsed with a haemorrhaging stomach ulcer. The day was not going well for Eicke.

Nonetheless, the British eventually withdrew from Bethune and formed a defensive line between Locon and La Paradis. *Totenkopf* was facing the 8th Lancashire Fusiliers, the 2nd Battalion of the Royal Norfolk Regiment and the 1st Battalion Royal Scots. All the British formations had been involved in heavy fighting for some days and they had been ordered to hold on as long as possible. Once again, the British

were determined to give *Totenkopf* a hard fight. On the left of *Totenkopf*'s advance, elements of the 2nd Regiment came up against C Company and the Headquarters Company of the 2nd Battalion Royal Norfolk Regiment, who had dug themselves in around a farmhouse outside the village of Le Paradis. These men checked *Totenkopf*'s advance, but were soon surrounded. The British had been ordered to hold on until dusk in order to buy as much time as possible. When their ammunition finally ran out at about 1715 hours, the Norfolk's commander, Major Ryder, ordered the 100 or so survivors of the 2nd Battalion to surrender. Thus, the British marched out under a white flag to surrender to the 14th Company of *Totenkopf*'s 1st Battalion of the 2nd Regiment, whose commander had been Bertling. The 14th

Left: A mortar team of the *Totenkopf* Division in action in France. The 8cm sGrW 34 was the mainstay of German close support weapons, and was widely used by all German units throughout the war.

Below: Eicke finally got his wish for action in France. *Totenkopf* moved forward to exploit the German success, only to meet the British counter-attack at Arras. Although successful, *Totenkopf* had a high casualty rate.

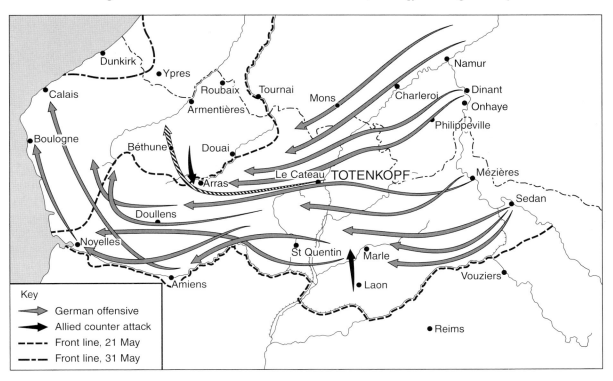

Company was commanded by *SS-Obersturmführer* (First Lieutenant) Fritz Knöchlein. Knöchlein marched his prisoners across the road and into a nearby barnyard. Albert Pooley of the 2nd Norfolks' recalled what happened:

> we turned off the dusty French road, through a gateway and into a meadow beside the buildings of a farm. I saw with one of the nastiest feelings I have ever had in my life two heavy machine guns inside the meadow … pointing at the head of our

Above: General Hoepner, commander of the 16th Panzer Corps, which included *Totenkopf* from 22 May onwards, in Dijon in 1940. He disliked Eicke and had little respect for the division or its activities.

column. The guns began to spit fire … for a few seconds the cries and the shrieks of our stricken men drowned the crackling of the guns. Men fell like grass before a scythe … I felt a searing pain and pitched forward … my scream of pain mingled with the cries of my mates, but even before I fell into the heap of dying men, the thought stabbed my brain 'If I ever get out of here, the swine that did this will pay for it.'

The massacre of the men of the Royal Norfolk Regiment was the most wanton act of brutality committed by the German Army during the French campaign. German machine gunners continued to fire into the Norfolks' bodies until the cries of the wounded had ceased. Knöchlein then had his men fix bayonets and finish off any men who showed the faintest sign of life. An hour later, he was satisfied that all the British soldiers were dead and the company moved off to rejoin the rest of the regiment. Incredibly, two men survived the massacre, Albert Pooley quoted above and William O'Callaghan. O'Callaghan, who was less badly wounded, managed to pull Pooley from the pile of corpses and the pair hid in a pigsty in a nearby farm. They were finally captured by the more merciful 251st Infantry Division. Pooley was true to his thoughts as he and his comrades were machine-gunned. The testimony of both survivors was instrumental in the prosecution of Knöchlein by a British military court in Hamburg in 1948. He was sentenced to death as a war criminal and hanged.

The men of *Totenkopf* had been imbued with a real sense of fanaticism throughout their training and indoctrination before the French campaign. This had shown itself in the recklessness and determination with which they carried out their attacks. There is little doubt that they had displayed considerable bravery in the fighting in France. Yet it had not brought them success in battle when they encountered British troops along La Bassée Canal. They had taken foolish risks and suffered disastrous casualties as a consequence. This frustration, coupled with the fanatical hatred of the enemy Eicke had so enthusiastically inculcated in his men, seems to have led Knöchlein to order the murder of the 97 men of the Royal Norfolk Regiment that were his prisoners.

Following the massacre, *Totenkopf* pushed forwards, pressing against the British withdrawing towards Dunkirk. The next day, Hoepner ordered *Totenkopf* to lead the attack against the new defensive line the British had established on the Lys canal. Fatigue, the heavy casualties already suffered and fierce British counterattacks forced Eicke's men onto the defensive. When his attack was called off at dusk, the division had advanced less than a quarter of a mile. Hoepner was angered by this lack of success and told Eicke to resume the attack the following morning. Fortunately, the British began to withdraw slowly. Hoepner's superior, General Hermann Hoth, ordered Eicke to pursue, but accurate British artillery fire stalled *Totenkopf*'s advance once again and the entire British rearguard managed to get away from the Germans. Eventually, elements of *Totenkopf*'s 1st Regiment linked up with the 16th Panzer Corps, but they were too slow to halt the bulk of the British forces withdrawing into the relative safety of the Dunkirk perimeter. The division was then ordered to halt, and thus its part in the first phase of the battle for France was complete.

THE DRIVE SOUTH

Totenkopf was briefly pulled out of the line and sent for a period of occupation duties around Boulougne. Meanwhile, news of the Le Paradis massacre spread through the neighbouring divisions and eventually reached the ears of Hoepner, who ordered a full investigation. Hoepner was determined to have Eicke dismissed if it could be proved that *Totenkopf* had been mistreating and even murdering prisoners. However, this investigation seems to have had no effect on either *Totenkopf* or Eicke. No charges were ever brought against Knöchlein and the only problem Eicke faced was to explain the incident away to Himmler by claiming somewhat weakly that the British had been using dumdum bullets. Some accounts claim that other SS officers in the division were so horrified by Knöchlein's actions that they wanted to challenge him to a duel. Certainly, Knöchlein never fought a duel with any SS officer, nor did the incident have any effect on his subsequent career in the SS. Given what most officers had experienced as concentration camp guards before the war, it is unlikely that any of them were particularly horrified by his actions. In the final days around

Dunkirk, interest in the incident faded quickly as the enormity of other events sunk in.

Totenkopf had taken quite a mauling in the 10 days between 19 and 29 May, suffering 1140 casualties, including 300 officers, which was a serious problem. Himmler was forced to send Eicke 300 half-trained officer cadets from Bad Tölz to keep the division in the field. Eicke was soon told to move southwards to participate in the final defeat of the French Army and the division took part in the pursuit of the French armies south of the Marne from 14 June onwards. Organised French resistance had collapsed by this time and any fighting that occurred was at the initiative of local French commanders. Near Dijon, the 5th Company of the 2nd Battalion of the 2nd Regiment fought a fierce engagement with Moroccan troops and the SS took no prisoners from soldiers they con-

Above: After the fall of France, large amounts of French equipment fell into German hands, which was used for a variety of tasks. Here a *Totenkopf* gun team train with a Puteaux mle 1937 4.7cm anti-tank gun.

sidered their racial inferiors. Indeed, during this period, the only French troops that managed to surrender to *Totenkopf* were white. Essentially, the drive south was one large mopping-up operation. According to the *Totenkopf* war diary, between 17 and 19 June, the division had taken 6088 prisoners at a cost of five killed and 13 wounded. The following day, the reconnaissance battalion took the surrender of 1300 French troops. Finally, on 22 June, the French Government surrendered and hostilities officially ended on 25 June 1940. *Totenkopf* was assigned occupation duties near the Spanish border.

PROVEN COMBAT SUCCESS

The French campaign proved that *Totenkopf*, the division made up of concentration camp guards, could perform creditably enough to be considered a competent military formation. *Totenkopf* troops had shown considerable courage and resilience in combat. Conversely, they had suffered extremely heavy casualties; in fact, there were 1152, slightly more than 10 per cent of the unit's combat strength. This was a product not only of *Totenkopf*'s bravery and tenacity, but also of the poor leadership of *Totenkopf*'s inexperienced officers, who took too many risks with their men's lives to achieve their objectives. The campaign

had also shown the division's propensity for brutality. The massacre at Le Paradis and the refusal to take Moroccan prisoners were products of the fanaticism and hatred of the enemy that Eicke had instilled in his troops. This may have produced feats of stupendous heroism, but it also led to acts of barbarism, which cannot do anything but detract from their achievements as soldiers.

Below: The spoils of war: members of the *Totenkopf* Division celebrate with champagne after Germany's lightning victory over France. It was a brief moment of rest, as soon they would be training for the invasion of Russia.

CHAPTER FOUR

NORTHERN THRUST

After months of hard training, *Totenkopf* was ready to take part in the invasion of the Soviet Union in June 1941. Driving towards Leningrad, the division found itself halted near Lake Ilmen, where it would be decimated by Soviet counter-attacks over the coming winter.

As *Totenkopf* settled down for a period of rest and rebuilding in the Bordeaux region, the possibility of invading Britain, for which the division was training, began to fade away. The summer of 1940 turned into autumn, Hitler turned his eyes eastwards, and the German High Command began to plan for Operation Barbarossa, the invasion of the Soviet Union. Meanwhile, the performance of the SS divisions in France convinced Hitler to allow Himmler to expand the *Waffen-SS* from three divisions to six. Not content simply to deal with the clashes that this brought between the SS and the army over manpower, Himmler also decided to rationalise the command structure of the *Waffen-SS*. Eicke held disproportionate influence within the organisation, despite his position as a mere divisional commander. As former commander of the concentration camp system, he used the *Totenkopf* units and stockpiles of weapons, vehicles and supplies within the camps as a vast reserve for the division. Himmler decided to break Eicke's hold on this massive pool of manpower and weapons, and use the Death's Head units as a source of replacements

for the entire SS. Although Eicke resisted, he was forced to accept a much-reduced role within the new and larger *Waffen-SS*.

TOTENKOPF REBUILT

Eicke used the year between the French campaign and the Russian campaign to strengthen the firepower of his division. He converted the motorised infantry regiments into self-contained *Kampfgruppen*, or battle groups, thus giving them a greater degree of independence and flexibility. *Totenkopf*'s flak capability was expanded and Eicke gained the long-promised allotment of enough 150-mm heavy artillery pieces to assemble a heavy battalion in *Totenkopf*'s artillery regiment. He established a motorised reserve battalion which in future would act as *Totenkopf*'s primary source of replacements, now that he had lost control of the *Totenkopfverbände* in the concentration camps.

Eicke trained the division as hard as ever and also introduced an extensive programme of political indoctrination. This contained the usual mixture of Nazi history and racial theory. The division was fed a steady diet of propaganda over the winter of 1940–41. How far it affected *Totenkopf*'s personnel is difficult to measure, but, given their behaviour in France and their future performance in the Soviet Union, it is reasonable to conclude that the constant exposure to

Left: The plains of Russia, 1941. A *Totenkopf* sniper armed with a Kar 98K with telescopic sight takes aim during the opening phases of Operation Barbarossa. He has goggles on his helmet to protect his eyes against the dust.

for the invasion of the Soviet Union. *Totenkopf*, which was part of the 7th Army, was instructed to be ready to move at a moment's notice. Leave was cancelled in the division on 5 May, implying to the men that something important was afoot. Finally, on 23 May 1941, Eicke was instructed to have the division ready to move by rail by 3 June. After frantic preparation on that day, the first elements of *Totenkopf* steamed out of the rail yards at Bordeaux towards the Soviet border. The men were virtually sealed in their cars for the entire journey and were only allowed out at selected stations. By the evening of 9 June, the last of the division's trains had arrived at their destination: Marienwerder in East Prussia. The division then moved to near the frontier of East Prussia and Soviet-occupied Lithuania.

For the Russian campaign, the division was attached to Erich Hoepner's 4th Panzer Group, which would be the vanguard of Field Marshal Wilhelm Ritter von Leeb's Army Group North. Hoepner's group, which contained 41st and 56th Panzer Corps led by Max Reinhardt and Erich von Manstein, respectively, would lead the attack through the Baltic states to Leningrad. Hoepner had a personal dislike of Eicke and did not think much of the division, having had it under his command in France. Thus he refused to designate *Totenkopf* for the first wave. Eicke would once again have to wait in reserve.

As the last SS reservists were drafted in to bring *Totenkopf* up to full strength, Eicke briefed his officers on the forthcoming war in the East. This new campaign, he claimed, was different; it was a life-and-death struggle between National Socialism and Jewish Bolshevism. It would be a ruthless and uncompromising ideological war. The Führer, Eicke continued, had therefore ordered that all political commissars attached to Red Army formations be shot immediately, regardless of the circumstances. Eicke ended by instructing his officers to be fanatical and merciless,

Eicke's theories on race and Nazi Germany's enemies had some impact.

During that French winter, the division switched to training specifically for combat in the Soviet Union. Exercises stressed fighting in forests and small villages under difficult weather conditions. Max Simon, the commander of the 1st Infantry Regiment, perfected the deployment of the motorised regiment, while the new operations officer, Heinz Lammerding, attended a number of special courses in tactical and logistical problems. Eicke also had him command regimental-sized battle groups in exercises. The gruelling pace was kept up through the spring of 1941 while the other SS divisions were sent to Greece. After the surrender of the Greek Army, Hitler ordered the resumption of preparations for Barbarossa and began the final stages of the build-up

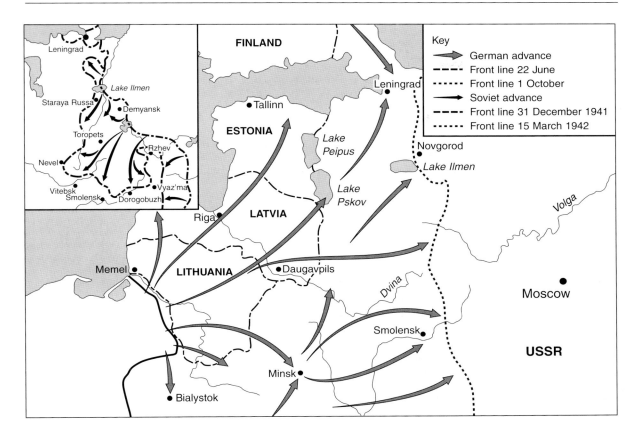

Above: A map showing the northern and central drives on Moscow and Leningrad in 1941. *Totenkopf* **ended up near Lake Ilmen, where the division was later involved in the Demyansk pocket (shown in the inset map) in 1942.**

and he reminded them that the Soviets had not signed the Geneva Convention and thus would not fight in a civilised manner – nor would any prisoners be treated correctly. *Totenkopf* would fight without mercy in the East for the fate of the German people.

THE OPENING OF BARBAROSSA

By early June 1941, the Wehrmacht had massed more than three million men and 3350 tanks in 149 divisions divided between three army groups, supported by 2770 aircraft. Before dawn on 22 June, they attacked across the Soviet border. The 4th Panzer Corps' first objective was the bridges across the Dvina River, which formed a formidable defensive barrier. Hoepner's group had control of the bridges by 26 June. The rapidity of the corps' progress – 320km (200 miles) in two days – dislocated the German advance, as the infantry divisions were left behind

and a gap had opened up between Manstein's 56th Panzer Corps and 16th Army to Manstein's south. Furthermore, the panzer drive towards the river had meant large Soviet formations had been bypassed. *Totenkopf* was therefore brought out of reserve and ordered eastwards to plug the gap and clear up any Soviet stragglers it met along the way.

The division crossed the border on 24/25 June, cleared the Lithuanian forests around Jurbarkas and then moved towards the Dvina. On 27 June, the Reconnaissance Battalion made the division's first serious contact with Soviet forces, which were beginning to re-form after the shock of the original

Above: *Totenkopf* **soldiers aboard a light 6x4 truck. Unlike the majority of the** *Wehrmacht* **divisions involved, all the** *Waffen-SS* **divisions committed to the start of Operation Barbarossa were motorised.**

German assault. The battalion was able to drive off the Soviet tanks without too much difficulty, but was somewhat shaken by the repeated and suicidal attacks launched by the Soviet infantry. The following day, Simon's 1st Infantry Regiment suffered a similar experience. Simon's men were also unnerved by the fanaticism of the Soviet troops, who fought to the death rather than surrender. It seemed incredible that isolated and demoralised groups of Soviet troops would fight on under these circumstances. Simon's straightforward solution was that these men were bandits and should be dealt with accordingly. Similarly, stories of Russian atrocities committed against captured Germans were also filtering back to the *Totenkopf* units. As a result, few Soviet prisoners were taken by the division as it drove eastwards.

Upon reaching the Dvina, *Totenkopf* was assigned to Manstein's 56th Panzer Corps and given the task of

guarding the corps' flank and maintaining contact with the 16th Army to the south. Hoepner's next objective was the Stalin Line, a string of fortifications running south from Lake Peipus, along the route Pskov–Ostrov–Opochka. Once the line had been cracked, Reinhardt's 41st Panzer Corps would drive on Leningrad, while Manstein's would move towards Lake Ilmen to cut the vital Leningrad-to-Moscow railway line. Initially, *Totenkopf's* advance went very well, but Soviet resistance from the badly mauled 21st Soviet Armoured Group stiffened and, at the village of Dagda, Simon's regiment again bore the brunt of the fighting, sustaining just over 100 casualties. The growing scale of Russian counterattacks, supported by tanks and artillery, forced *Totenkopf* onto the defensive. Only with Stuka support did Eicke manage to resume the advance.

On 5 July, Manstein's 56th Panzer Corps paused to regroup in preparation for the assault on the Stalin line. *Totenkopf* was to pass southwards of the Soviet defensive line to cut off any Soviet formations driven back by 56th Panzer Corps' other divisions, 8th Panzer Division and 3rd Motorised Division. When the assault opened on 6 July, *Totenkopf* discovered the fortifications were much denser in its sector than anticipated and the division struggled to clear the lines of bunkers, wire and minefields defended by determined Soviet troops. Losses again were high and, most seriously, Eicke was amongst the casualties. Close to midnight, his staff car ran over a mine, seriously wounding Eicke – his right foot was shattered – and his driver. Before being removed to a rear area hospital, Eicke appointed Matthias Kleinheister-kamp, the head of the 3rd Infantry Regiment, commander of the division in his absence.

The Soviets, determined not to lose the key town of Opochka, threw everything they could into the battles, including monster 152-mm gun-armed 52-ton KV-II tanks. The *Totenkopf* anti-tank gunners again discovered that their 37-mm Pak 35/36s were totally inadequate against such targets; the only hope was to shoot off these beasts' tracks and allow the infantry to finish the immobilised KV-IIs on foot. *Totenkopf* and the 30th Infantry Division from the 16th Army finally entered the town on 11 July and the fighting began to subside. The losses, as ever, had been high: 82 officers and 1626 men killed, wounded or missing. This was nearly 10 per cent of the unit's combat strength. Manstein was extremely critical of this high casualty rate, given the division's limited territorial gains. With the Stalin Line breached, Reinhardt could drive on Leningrad, while Manstein's corps would move towards Lake Ilmen. *Totenkopf* was taken out of the line for a period in reserve.

However, as the 56th Panzer Corps became entangled with further desperate Soviet resistance, Hoepner soon ordered the division back into action.

On 19 July, Manstein placed *Totenkopf* on his right flank and, at the same time, a new divisional commander arrived for *Totenkopf*. Himmler had decided to appoint *Brigadeführer* Georg Keppler to lead *Totenkopf* until Eicke recovered. Keppler was an experienced soldier and had led the crack *Verfügungs* Division regiment *Der Führer* in France. However, he was about to lead the division through some of the hardest fighting in 1941.

Keppler was given the task of protecting Manstein's flank and thus had to take *Totenkopf* into the dense forests and swamps southwest of Lake Ilmen. The Russians excelled at close-quarter fighting under these difficult conditions. The gains the division made as the men struggled forwards during the day were often lost as the Russians counterattacked at night. This ensured that the frontline units never had a decent night's sleep. More seriously, *Totenkopf's* strength continued to be whittled away by the constant attacks, while the Russians seemed to have an inexhaustible supply of manpower.

LAKE ILMEN

After 10 days of this, *Totenkopf* had reached the Luga Line, the fortification system that stretched from the western tip of Lake Ilmen to the Gulf of Finland. This was the last Soviet line before Leningrad. *Totenkopf* was detached from Manstein's corps and added to the 16th Army commanded by General Wiktorin. Keppler had the task of attacking the positions on the Mshaga River. It was hard going when the assault opened on 10 August. The division's artillery was stuck way behind the main advance in the network of swamps and was without air support. The Soviets, by contrast, had their artillery well sighted. On top of this, *Totenkopf's* communications were being tapped and its rear area harassed by partisan units. Supported by Stuka dive-bombers, the *Totenkopf* infantry established a firm bridgehead across the river in the face of suicidal Russian resistance. *Totenkopf* positions were charged time and time again throughout the night. Then, at daybreak, the counterattacks ceased and *Totenkopf* once again began cautiously to probe the Russian positions. Wiktorin

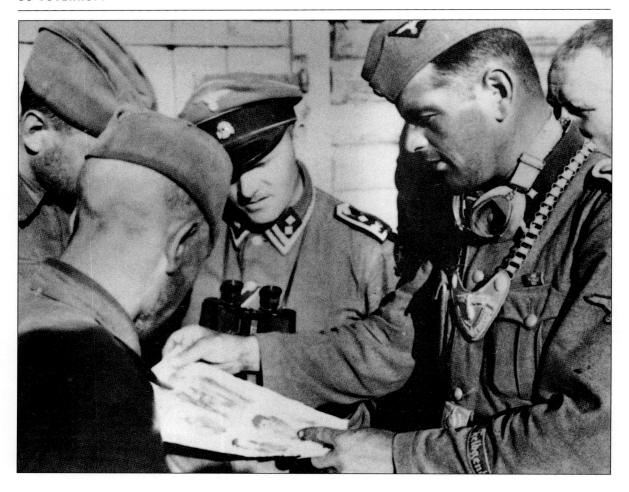

then ordered the division to guard the flank of 28th Army Corps, essentially to absorb wave after wave of Soviet counterattacks. Keppler was not overly pleased with *Totenkopf* being used as 'a punching bag'.

VOROSHILOV'S OFFENSIVE

This role did not last for long, as the supreme commander of the Soviet North-Western Front, Marshal Klimenti Voroshilov, launched a massive counteroffensive, aiming to split Army Group North and Army Group Centre. The Soviet 34th Army smashed into the German 10th Army Corps south of Lake Ilmen. The commander of Army Group North, Ritter von Leeb, responded by detaching 56th Panzer Corps and *Totenkopf*, and sending them to support 10th Army

Above: *Totenkopf* **officers confer in northern Russia in August–September 1941. In the late summer of 1941 the division was involved in bitter fighting around Lake Ilmen, trying to clear the forests of Soviet troops.**

Corps. Keppler had great problems extracting *Totenkopf*, however, because of Soviet counterattacks and the uncooperative behaviour of *Totenkopf*'s neighbouring divisions.

Manstein intended to absorb Voroshilov's attacks with 10th Army Corps, while *Totenkopf* and 3rd Motorised Division hit the Soviet 34th Army's flank. This duly occurred on 19 August and *Totenkopf* was soon enjoying massive success on the first day, taking 785 prisoners and large quantities of matériel.

Right: A junior officer seen wearing the divisional symbol on both lapels. He carries a holstered P08 pistol, map case and binoculars, and has his machine pistol – probably an MP28 – slung behind his back.

Manstein ordered the immediate pursuit of the retreating Soviet troops. The division managed to seize the bridges across the Polist River just south of Lake Ilmen and thus cut off the 34th Army's retreat. By 20 August, all organised Soviet resistance had ceased and the destruction of the trapped Russians began. On 21 August, *Totenkopf* captured more prisoners than it done in the entire French campaign. Overall, eight Red Army divisions had been destroyed. Manstein arrived at Keppler's headquarters to praise the division's performance.

SOVIET ADVANTAGE

Strategically, however, the Soviet position was stronger. Manstein's counterstroke had meant that the rest of Army Group North had remained static, allowing the Soviets to reinforce Leningrad's defences. Furthermore, a deadly war of attrition was going on; the Soviets' almost unlimited pool of manpower allowed them constantly to counterattack and wear down the Germans, who did not have such prodigious resources of personnel.

Totenkopf and 3rd Motorised drove east against steadily stiffening Soviet resistance, but the *Totenkopf* advance stalled in the face of unusually active Soviet air power, which caused considerable damage to the division's vehicles. On 28 August, Manstein ordered *Totenkopf* to cross the Pola River, but the division's efforts were hampered by repeated Soviet infantry attacks and heavy downpours that turned the Russian roads into quagmires. The following day, Keppler pleaded that his exhausted and much-weakened division could not be expected to attack again; with 4853 dead and insufficient replacements, *Totenkopf* sustained more losses than either other division in the corps. Manstein agreed to postpone the attack and promised to relieve the division as soon as possible. Yet the continued Red Army attacks allowed them no respite. The weather improved on 5 September and

Totenkopf engineers of Kleinheisterkamp's 3rd Regiment managed to get two battalions across the Pola.

The weather improved again and the Germans were able to resume their general advance, although progress was slow across the minefields and booby traps strewn in the wake of the retreating Soviet formations. The offensive faltered then halted in the face of further Soviet counteroffensives in the Demyansk area on 11/12 September. The division dug in and waited, and on the 18th the Russian attacks began. Wave after wave of infantry charged *Totenkopf*'s positions and then ceased abruptly at dusk.

The division then enjoyed a brief period of quiet and during this lull, on 21 September, Eicke returned

to his division and received a four-hour briefing from Keppler and Lammerding before Keppler flew back to Germany. Eicke, still using a stick, was horrified by the state of his men. The division had constantly been in action in the swamps and forests around Ilmen and it showed. Eicke swiftly directed energy to ensuring that the division received decent replacements and was withdrawn from the line. However, before he had time to achieve anything, the division was embroiled in another Soviet counter-offensive, one of a scale beyond anything yet experienced by the division.

THE SOVIET COUNTER-OFFENSIVE AND LUSHNO

Totenkopf was transferred to the 2nd Army Corps after Manstein had been transferred south and, on 22 September, corps headquarters warned Eicke that fresh Soviet units were being deployed opposite his divisions and that there had been an increase in Soviet patrolling and reconnaissance. Soviet artillery bombardment and air attacks also increased. Soviet infantry began to probe *Totenkopf*'s northern flank and discovered a gap between it and the neighbouring 30th Infantry Division. *Totenkopf* was strung along a 24-km (15-mile) front; Simon's regiment was positioned to the south and Kleinheisterkamp's 3rd Infantry Regiment was to the north, with the village of Lushno at the far northern tip of his regiment's positions. It was here that the main concentration of the Soviet attack would come.

At noon on 24 September, the attack began. Wave after wave of Soviet infantry broke on the *Totenkopf* positions and eventually broke over them. At Lushno, two Soviet regiments supported by 20 tanks overran the positions of the 3rd Regiment's 2nd Battalion and forced the survivors into confused retreat. The situation was only stabilised by the courage of the 2nd Company of the Tank-Destroyer Battalion and the *Totenkopf* artillery batteries behind Lushno firing over open sights into the charging Russians. Slightly to the

Left: A haunted-looking *Hauptsturmführer* of the *Totenkopf* Division in the Soviet Union in 1941, with a camouflage face mask on his helmet. The casualty rate of junior officers in the fighting around Lushno was very high.

north of the village was the anti-tank battery of *SS-Sturmmann* (Corporal) Fritz Christen, which bore the brunt of a massive armoured assault, including the excellent T-34 tank and massive KV-II tanks. During the first encounter, he saw his entire platoon killed, but Christen remained at his gun, knocked out six tanks and drove off the attack. Meanwhile, the concentrated fire of the artillery had broken up the Russian attacks and Eicke ordered a counterattack that evening which retook the village.

The expected Soviet counterstroke came at 0500 hours the following day. The SS men were better prepared this time, although the T-34 tanks now appearing were impervious to their 37-mm anti-tank guns. The corpses piled up in front of the German positions in the face of concentrated artillery, machine-gun and small arms fire. This time *Totenkopf* did not give up ground, despite half-hourly Soviet attacks. The Russians resorted to ever more bizarre tactics. An engineer unit dug in behind a minefield were surprised to be attacked by a herd of pigs, which had been driven across the field by the Russians in an effort to clear it.

The battle reached its peak on 26 and 27 September, as *Totenkopf* endured a continuous 48-hour assault by everything the Soviets could spare. Again, the main weight of the attack was at Lushno and on the 3rd Regiment, which had been fighting continuously without relief and re-supply. The 2nd Battalion had lost all its officers and yet, with only 150 men left in action, it managed to launch a counterattack and retake the village on the night 26/27 September. As has been noted, the 37-mm guns were useless against the Soviet T-34s and the 50-mm Pak 38 was only effective at 500m (540yds). Thus, the *Totenkopf* men had to take on the Soviet armour on foot using satchel charges, mines and Molotov cocktails to disable them. One such squad, led by engineer *Hauptsturmführer* Max Seela, destroyed seven T-34s in this manner on 26 September.

On 27 September, the Soviets committed the equivalent of three divisions and 100 tanks against *Totenkopf*. Eicke scoured the supply and support units for men to throw into the line, and armed and moved

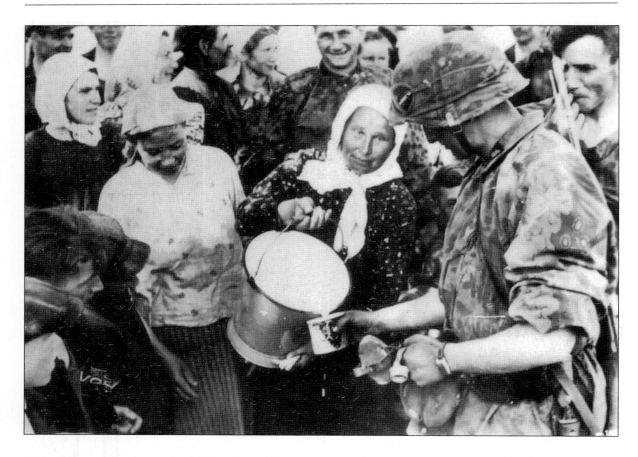

his HQ unit up to act as a last-ditch reserve if necessary. Lushno changed hands four times that day. When the SS men finally drove the Soviets out of the village, they were astonished to find Fritz Christen crouched behind his anti-tank gun, which he had manned alone for nearly three days. Around him were the 13 tanks that he had personally destroyed and the corpses of 100 Soviet troops he had killed. Eicke recommended him for the Knight's Cross, which Christen received personally from Hitler. Christen was the first and youngest SS enlistee to receive the award. The extraordinary resistance of Christen and the division as a whole showed a willingness to fight against appalling odds and this characterised *Totenkopf*'s performance throughout the war. Eicke's indoctrination and the division's fanaticism had its uses.

Above: As the Germans moved through the Baltic States, they were greeted as liberators by the majority of the population, as demonstrated by these Latvian women. The *Waffen-SS* recruited heavily from the Baltic States.

Right: *Totenkopf* soldiers in a village near Staraya Russa in the Demyansk pocket. Along with elements of the 18th Motorised Division, the *Totenkopf* endured some of the toughest fighting of the encirclement around this area.

DESPERATE FIGHTING

The defensive victory left *Totenkopf* much weakened. Eicke estimated that it had suffered 6610 casualties and only received 2500 replacements since the start of Barbarossa, and its equipment and vehicles had suffered similarly. Yet, once more, the division was ordered to advance. With regard to offensive action,

however, *Totenkopf* was a spent force and when, 16km (10miles) east of Lushno, the division hit new Russian defensive positions, it ground to a halt almost at once. Eicke's commanders were repeatedly warning him that their units were capable of little more than defensive action and soon they would not be capable of even that. All across the front, the German offensive was drawing to halt; importantly, at Moscow, the German assault had also stalled. *Totenkopf* and rest of the 16th Army began to dig in for the winter. Despite Eicke's pleas for relief, the success of the division meant that *Totenkopf*, despite much of the army's dislike of Eicke and his formation, had to stay in the line. It had gained a reputation for reliability and occupied a key position and therefore Army Group North could not afford to lose it.

Right: A *Totenkopf* **squad brings vital ammunition forward on a sled in the Demyansk pocket. The** *Luftwaffe* **did a reasonable job of supplying the defenders, but food and ammunition were still strictly rationed.**

In December 1941, the German drive eastwards finally stalled on the outskirts of Moscow, as the Soviet Marshal Georgi Zhukov launched a massive counter-attack with fresh crack Siberian divisions headed by massed T-34 tanks. The exhausted Army Group Centre fell back and the German position did not stabilise until mid-January 1942, in the wake of Hitler's no-retreat order. The Soviet counteroffensive was not, however, limited to the Moscow front. The Soviets assembled the 11th and 34th Armies and the 1st Shock Army for a massive offensive against the German forces south of Lake Ilmen, in an attempt to split Army Group North from Army Group Centre. In front of this planned drive lay 16th Army's 10th Corps and 2nd Corps, part of which was the *Totenkopf* Division. Eicke's forward observers and patrols noticed the build-up opposite their positions, and the division and its neighbours worked frantically to improve their positions.

FRESH SOVIET ATTACK

The attack came on the night 7/8 January 1942 in the midst of a blizzard, during which the temperature had dropped to below −40 degrees Celsius. The offensive directed against Army Group North's southern flank glanced against *Totenkopf*'s front and smashed into the division's neighbours, the 30th and 290th Infantry divisions. The 290th was utterly destroyed and the Soviets drove about 32km (20miles) into the rear of 10th Army Corps. Meanwhile, the Soviet 11th Army to the north drove into the rear of the 2nd and 10th Army Corps, and the Soviet 1st Shock Army drove upwards along the Lovat River in an effort to encircle the 16th Army. The 16th Army reacted by drawing a number of units from *Totenkopf*, much to Eicke's displeasure, and sent them to stiffen the areas of the front that threatened to collapse. Five battalions from *Totenkopf*, including the reconnaissance and engineer battalions and part of the artillery

regiment, were hurried north on 9 January, while Eicke was also forced to send two battalions south to bolster this flank. Field Marshal Leeb reckoned that the encirclement of the 16th Army was only a matter of time and requested Hitler to be allowed to withdraw the army to prevent it being cut off and destroyed. Hitler rejected the request and told the 16th Army to stand and fight. On receiving this reply, Leeb asked to be relieved and was replaced by Colonel General Georg von Küchler.

Meanwhile, the Soviets constricted the pocket around the town of Demyansk containing the 16th Army and, by 8 February, the Soviets had enclosed 2nd and 10th Army Corps, trapping the 12th, 30th, 32nd, 123rd and remnants of 290th Infantry divisions, plus the core of *Totenkopf*. The Russians could field 15 fresh infantry divisions against the exhausted and weakened Germans. Göring, the head of the

Above: *Totenkopf* **personnel await the next Soviet attack on their position. They have managed to procure reasonable winter clothing, which provides some camouflage. The nearest man is armed with an Erma EMP machine pistol.**

Right: These members of *Totenkopf* **seen in the Demyansk pocket are wearing the standard** *Wehrmacht* **greatcoat with blankets wrapped round them. They are carrying ammunition boxes and belts for the squad's machine gun.**

Luftwaffe, told Hitler that he could supply the 95,000 men in the pocket by air and Hitler therefore ordered the trapped divisions not to try to break out to the west.

The senior officer in the pocket was General Walter Brockdorff-Ahlefeldt; he broke *Totenkopf* into two regimental battle groups, which he deployed where the fighting was toughest. The larger group

was a mixture of SS and army troops from the 290th Infantry Division, under Eicke's command. Brockdorff-Ahlefeldt placed this group on the western edge of the pocket to ensure that the gap between his command and the German front line was not widened. The second battle group, which came under Max Simon's command, was placed on the northeastern side of the pocket, which faced severe pressure and threatened to collapse. Throughout February and early March, *Totenkopf* was under constant pressure, yet the men did not retreat from their positions while fighting in chest-deep snow and in temperatures that averaged –30 degrees Celsius.

SUCCESS OF THE *LUFTWAFFE*

The *Luftwaffe* managed to re-supply the pocket quite well. They had estimated that 200 tonnes were required to maintain the pocket and, at their peak, the *Luftwaffe* was actually bringing in 300 tonnes, although this dropped off to only half the required amount as the weather worsened. The battle to eliminate the pocket reached its climax in the last week of February. The bulk of the Soviet effort was directed against Eicke's western part of western sector and at times his command was cut into isolated individual pockets. Yet the *Totenkopf* men refused to retreat: if a position was overcome, it was only at the expense of all the defenders. The fanatical resistance took its toll by the third week in February. Eicke's entire battle group defending an 13-km (8-mile) front was down to 36 officers, 191 NCOs and 1233 men. Yet the Soviet attack continued unabated and, on 28 February, Eicke lost contact with his neighbouring units. Still *Totenkopf* held on, despite the fact that Soviets had committed their remaining reserves in a final effort to crush the pocket.

By March, the Russian attacks on Eicke's western sector had subsided as the continuous fanatical assaults finally also took their toll on the Soviet divisions. The crack Soviet 7th Guards Division had been virtually annihilated. *Totenkopf*, too, was in similar condition; the division was on the verge of destruction. By the beginning of March, however, preparations were being made for an attempt to relieve the pocket. The commander of the operation, Lieutenant General Walter von Seydlitz, had assembled five divisions to punch through Soviet lines to relieve the Demyansk pocket. Hitler agreed that German troops in the pocket should also attack westwards in an effort to assist Seydlitz's relief attempt and therefore some of the best units available were placed on the western side of the Demyansk pocket.

RELIEF ATTEMPT

The relief attempt was launched on 21 March and, for two days, Seydlitz's divisions made good progress. However, Soviet resistance soon stiffened and, by 28 March, the advance had stalled. From this point on, Seydlitz's forces pushed forwards slowly through the Russian defensive network east of the pocket. The proposed breakout westwards was continually postponed. Only on 14 April did Seydlitz feel that he had advanced far enough to order Eicke to attempt to link up with him. Unfortunately, the launching of so-called Operation Gangway coincided with the first spring thaw and thus the SS and army soldiers had to fight through chest-deep swamps which only days before had been frozen and easily crossed. The fighting in these conditions was particularly bitter. Eicke's battle group pushed forwards, averaging little more than a mile a day until, on 20 April, a company from *Totenkopf*'s tank-destroyer battalion reached the River Lovat. The following day, other units reached the company and, on 22 April, a bridgehead was established between the troops in the Demyansk pocket and the rest of Army Group North.

Eicke was awarded the Knight's Cross, and subsequently the Oak Leaves, and promoted to *SS-Obergruppenführer* for *Totenkopf*'s achievement of holding on and battering its way out of the pocket, which contributed significantly to the stabilisation of the German position around Lake Ilmen. Hitler personally awarded him the medal that June, and the Führer declared that *Totenkopf* was largely responsible for the survival of the Demyansk pocket. Eleven other men from the division received the Knight's Cross for their performance between January and March 1942.

Eicke's division, however, was in an appalling condition. Eicke wrote to Himmler that he needed 10,000 replacements or the division withdrawn from the front if it was to continue to function. The men of the

Above: A *Totenkopf* soldier seen on the Eastern Front with a Kar 98k rifle, tin of rations, bayonet, sheet music and an accordion. Such a musician would be popular among other members of his squad.

division were exhausted both physically and mentally by their constant fighting.

The condition of *Totenkopf*'s troops was illustrated by a report sent to Max Simon by Dr Eckert of the 2nd Battalion of Simon's regiment. Of the men he examined, he judged just under two-thirds were unfit for further military service. Some, he continued, were as in as bad a physical state as the concentration camp inmates he had seen during his tour of duty in the camp system, which, as Charles Sydnor notes, was 'a most revealing comment in several respects'. On average, the rest of the men had lost 9kg (20lbs) in weight and were listless and weak. Himmler dismissed this and other similar reports forwarded to him and reassured Eicke that the return of warm weather and availability of fresh vegetables would quickly restore the rest of the division. The performance of the division around Lushno meant that the German authorities, including Himmler and Hitler, were even less inclined to withdraw *Totenkopf* for rest and refitting. Thus, it had to endure an extended period in the line, even after the relief of the Demyansk pocket.

CORPS COMMANDER

The pocket remained a precarious bulge into the Soviet lines and, in May 1942, Hitler gave Eicke a 'corps' command with the instruction to hold open its western end. Eicke's corps consisted of 14,000 survivors from the six divisions that had been encircled and terribly mauled in Demyansk. They were defending a 72-km (45-mile) long front, which all military authorities agreed was impossible. Colonel General Busch, the commander of the 16th Army, agreed with Eicke's analysis that the situation was hopeless unless *Totenkopf* was heavily reinforced with at least 5000 replacements.

All *Totenkopf* received was 3000 ill-trained reservists from Germany. The hoped-for guns and equipment never arrived, as Himmler could see that the division was shattered and was already planning a new *Totenkopf* division in Germany. The division at Demyansk received no new artillery or vehicles, while their opponents were liberally equipped with both. The Soviets resumed their offensive in May 1942 and

Right: A PzKpfw III Model H of the *Totenkopf*'s new light tank battalions. While Simon's troops were being killed in Demyansk in late 1942, the division was being effectively rebuilt in France as a panzergrenadier division.

were repulsed with difficulty. However, by the summer of that year, the Soviet build-up was such that it was apparent that a large offensive was imminent. Yet Eicke was ordered home in June by Himmler for a period of leave. He handed the division over to Simon. While Eicke took the opportunity to protest to Himmler face to face about the treatment of his men, Simon was confronted with the total destruction of the original *Totenkopf* division.

In July, as the great German summer offensive in southern Russia pushed towards the Caucasus, the Soviets began to try to constrict the corridor into the Demyansk salient, prompting Simon to plead for the relief of his battered and demoralised division. Although *Totenkopf* continued to endure, the continued attacks whittled away the division's strength. Simon predicted that the utter destruction of *Totenkopf* was only a matter of time. In the face of continued Soviet offensives throughout July, *Totenkopf*'s strength was continually eroded.

The desperation of the situation is well illustrated by Simon's refusal to obey an order from Brockdorff-Ahlefeldt; it was the first time that *Totenkopf* had disobeyed a direct command from the army. When a key town in Simon's sector was lost at the cost of two companies of SS men, the corridor into the pocket was once again at risk. Brockdorff-Ahlefeldt told Simon to retake it. Simon told him that *Totenkopf* had taken 532 casualties that afternoon and that, if the army wanted the town retaken, one of its units could do it. This went unpunished and an army unit attempted and, to Simon's delight, failed to retake the town.

The Russian attacks finally ceased on 30 July and the corridor remained open. Simon again protested that his command could not hold on much longer, as he had only 51 officers and 2685 men to defend the 41-km (25-mile) long northern side of the salient. In a letter to Eicke on 2 August, Simon confessed to

having lost hope. *Totenkopf* could not endure much longer. Eicke was shocked by Simon's letter and told Hitler 'that the army would hold Demyansk to the last drop of SS blood' and demanded to be returned to his command. Hitler refused his request.

TOTENKOPF RELIEVED

The Soviets attacked again in August and, once again, *Totenkopf* bore the brunt of the fighting. Simon was certain that the division could not last much longer. The core of the division, the 1st and 3rd Infantry Regiments, was down to a combined strength of fewer than 1000 men and Simon pointed out that, if the

division was to be rebuilt, it needed a cadre of experienced infantry men and that the division had to be withdrawn. Of course, it was not. In the last days of August, in the face of repeated Soviet counterattacks, *Totenkopf* was losing just fewer than 100 men a day. Finally, the constant lobbying of Eicke and Himmler prompted Hitler to issue a directive on 28 August for the complete reconstruction of the division. He agreed to the withdrawal of its remnants in order to rebuild the formation as a panzer grenadier division. To quote Charles Sydnor again: 'To Max Simon and the human skeletons he commanded around Demyansk, Hitler's decision was an 11th hour reprieve'.

CHAPTER FIVE

TOTENKOPF REBORN

Rebuilt in France after the heavy losses of 1942, *Totenkopf* was now upgraded to a panzer grenadier division, ready to take part in the next stage of Hitler's struggle in the East, which, after Kursk, would see the division used once more as a 'fire brigade' unit, shoring up the line.

The bitter attrition of the *Totenkopf* division from February to October 1942 in the Demyansk pocket led Himmler to decide that the division needed to be completely rebuilt. From May 1942, the division in the pocket was refused any decent quantity of replacement manpower and equipment, as these were required for the new formation. Eicke was sent on leave in June 1942, but soon immersed himself in the reconstruction of his division, while pleading for the relief of his men at Demyansk. Even when he was allowed to return to his command, he was forced to commute back to Germany weekly to supervise the ongoing work on the new panzer grenadier unit.

At the end of October 1942, the remnants of *Totenkopf* were finally pulled out of the line on the Eastern Front and put on trains for Germany. Lammerding, the operations officer, assembled them at Paderborn and sent them to Bordeaux in the south of France, where Eicke and his staff were preparing the new division. Eicke had been made a number of promises by both Hitler and Himmler about the strength of the division and, indeed, on paper, the

Left: Generalfeldmarschall **Erich von Manstein leaves his command post. Manstein, commander of Army Group South during Operation** *Zitadelle*, **held** *Totenkopf* **in very high regard as a fighting unit.**

new *Totenkopf* panzer grenadier division appeared to be one of the most powerful formations in the German Army.

CHANGES TO THE DIVISION

Hitler approved the formation of a tank battalion for *Totenkopf*, equipped largely with PzKpfw IIIs and PzKpfw IVs. In October, however, he expanded this to an armoured regiment, including a battalion of assault guns. More importantly, the Führer added a company of Tiger tanks to *Totenkopf*'s theoretical inventory. The division's anti-aircraft capability was increased (a tacit acknowledgment that Germany no longer controlled the skies) and the core of the panzer grenadier – that is, motorised infantry component – was to be based around SS 9th Infantry Regiment, which was renamed *Thule*. The tank-destroyer battalion finally lost its 37mm Pak 35/36s and received, as well as the 50mm Pak 38, a number of the new and extremely potent 75mm Pak 40 guns. It was an impressive order of battle on paper, but, unfortunately for Eicke, in reality *Totenkopf* was nowhere near as formidable.

At first, Eicke, as ever, was unimpressed by the division's replacement manpower. He was convinced they needed to be virtually trained from scratch, or they would be torn to pieces on the Eastern Front by

the Soviet troops. This Eicke could rectify if he had sufficient time. The most pressing and serious problem was his lack of equipment and vehicles. By the beginning of November, he had fewer than half the vehicles required, and not enough fuel to train his crews. Even by the beginning of January 1943, *Totenkopf* had not yet received its Tigers. Training was disrupted by *Totenkopf*'s participation in the occupation of Vichy France in the wake of the Allied invasion of North Africa, Operation Torch. On 9 November 1942, the division was ordered to the Mediterranean between Beziers and Montpelier, and the move used up all the precious fuel that Eicke and his staff had carefully stored. The division remained on coastal

defence duty until 18 December, when Eicke's pleas to be allowed to resume training his men were finally heeded, and a reserve infantry division was found to take over from *Totenkopf*.

Eicke was alarmed by the impending dispatch of his division to the Eastern Front and begged Himmler to postpone the move until *Totenkopf* was ready. Eicke warned that, given the state of equipment and training, sending *Totenkopf* into combat at that point would result in its rapid destruction. Himmler had no wish to see one of the most prestigious formations meeting the fate that Eicke so vividly anticipated, and thus met Hitler and successfully persuaded him to put back *Totenkopf*'s transfer to Russia.

Left: A *Totenkopf* tank rolls through the outskirts of Kharkov in March 1943. Working closely with the *Das Reich* Division, *Totenkopf* was instrumental in achieving this rare German success.

Himmler then contacted Eicke and told him that he had only an extra four weeks, as the division could not be spared from the deteriorating German position on the Eastern Front. Eicke used the time as only he could and drove his division from dawn until midnight in an effort to bring the men up to the requisite standard. He made good use of the division's veterans of the Eastern Front, who lectured on Soviet military techniques and armoured tactics. The delay also allowed Eicke to make up the deficits in equipment using his remarkable requisitioning skills. Additionally, just over half of the promised Tiger tanks arrived, and the crews had a brief period to familiarise themselves with their new weapons.

The division and its equipment boarded some 120 trains at Bordeaux on 30 January 1943, and spent two weeks travelling across the Reich before they detrained at Kiev, the main railhead for the German Army in the southern Soviet Union. On arriving in Kiev, Eicke was ordered eastwards to Poltava, to join up with the other crack SS divisions, *Leibstandarte* and *Das Reich* (the renamed *Verfügungs* Division), which had also been reconstituted as panzer grenadier formations and, like *Totenkopf*, now boasted formidable armoured forces. Together with these elite formations, *Totenkopf* would become part of *SS-Obergruppenführer* Paul Hausser's 1st SS Panzer Corps.

The hasty return had been necessitated by the disastrous winter that the Wehrmacht had endured on the Eastern Front in 1942–43. General von Paulus's 6th Army had been encircled and cut off at Stalingrad by a well-executed Soviet counterstroke in November and the 6th Army had been steadily reduced ever since, the pocket finally surrendering in early February. The Soviets had followed up their success at Stalingrad with a massive winter offensive launched on 12 January 1943. The German Army in the south was knocked back some 480km (300miles) almost to the Dnieper, losing the city of Kharkov in the process.

It was this city that Hitler wanted to use his elite panzer corps to recapture.

The Commander in Chief of Army Group South, Field Marshal von Manstein, had other ideas. He preferred to use the 1st SS Panzer Corps as the upper part of a pincer movement which would encircle and destroy the Soviet armies pushing towards the Dnieper. Hermann Hoth's 4th Panzer Army would be the southern part of the thrust. Hitler refused to countenance Manstein's plan, despite the field marshal's best efforts to persuade him. The Führer wanted a prestigious victory, and had his heart set on the recapture of Kharkov, an important communications centre. Manstein had resigned himself to carrying out the Führer's wishes when Eicke unintentionally came to his rescue.

TOTENKOPF BOGGED DOWN

Totenkopf had been making reasonable time on the journey between Kiev and Poltava, but the impatient Eicke wanted to speed their progress. On 17 February, he ordered the division off the main road onto the frozen countryside in order to up the pace and for a while that day the division enjoyed good going over the rock-hard ground. That night, the temperature rose above freezing and the ground began to thaw; Eicke and the division's transport suddenly sunk deep into the mud. He was forced to radio Hausser that *Totenkopf* was stuck fast 40km (25miles) from their destination. Hitler had to therefore postpone his attack on Kharkov because Hausser's corps could not hope to succeed without *Totenkopf*, and he reluctantly approved Manstein's counteroffensive.

When the division was finally hauled out of the mud and reached the rest of the corps, the attack was launched almost at once. Hoth's divisions in the south hit and knocked backwards the vanguard of the Soviet 6th and 1st Guard Armies, who retreated northwards. At the same time, *Totenkopf* and *Das Reich*, who were leading the 1st SS Panzer Corps, drove into the rear of the Soviet 6th Army and the Soviet retreat rapidly turned into a disaster. *Totenkopf's* tanks and armoured vehicles destroyed columns of trucks filled with fleeing Soviet troops. As the Soviet's T-34s ran out of petrol and coughed to a halt, Eicke's panzers destroyed them where they sat. The Soviet escape was cut off by *Totenkopf*'s 1st Panzer Grenadier Regiment, commanded by *SS-Obersturmbannführer* Otto Baum, and elements of *Das Reich* who had sped ahead and now formed a line across the Soviet route of retreat. To the south, the rest of *Totenkopf* fanned out across the steppe to finish off what resistance was left. By 1 March, it was all over. Hausser's Panzer Corps and Hoth's 4th Panzer Army had destroyed the bulk of two Soviet armies and reversed – albeit temporarily – the course of the war in the east. The Germans had captured or destroyed almost 615 tanks, 400 howitzers and artillery pieces, and 600 anti-tank guns. Admittedly, many Soviet soldiers were able to escape on foot due to the German's lack of supporting infantry. Nonetheless, 23,000 were killed and 9000 captured. Manstein's counterattack stabilised the German front in the southern Soviet Union and meant that the Germans now had time to plan and refit for the offensives in the forthcoming summer.

THE DEATH OF EICKE

This massive victory was not without cost. On the afternoon of 26 February 1943, as the pursuit streaked across the steppe and *Totenkopf*'s regiments were increasingly strung out, headquarters lost contact with the division's panzer regiment. Unable to make radio contact, Eicke decided to find it himself. He took off from his field headquarters in his single-engine Fieseler Storch scout plane to see if it could be

Below: Street fighting in Kharkov. Hausser's decision to storm the city rather than encircle and besiege it as Manstein had ordered him to do cost the *Waffen-SS* divisions many additional casualties.

Right: *Totenkopf* **tank commanders pause for a cigarette break during the fighting for Kharkov in early 1943. The operation gave the tank crews a chance to put their training and new equipment to the test.**

located from the air. At about 1630 hours, his pilot spotted a company of the Panzer Regiment's tanks ahead in and around a small Russian village called Michailovka. What he did not notice, however, was that Soviet troops were dug in nearby. So, as the plane circled to come in to land, it was met by a fusillade of shots from the Soviet positions, which tore the fragile plane apart. It crashed midway between the German and Soviet positions. Immediate German attempts to recover the body from the burning wreckage failed in the face of withering Soviet fire. As darkness fell, the efforts ceased and reinforcements were called up so they could try again in the morning. At 0515 hours the following day, an assault group commanded by *SS-Hauptsturmführer* Lino Masarie and made up of a motorcycle company, two assault guns and three tanks covered by artillery, went in and drove the Soviets from their positions to recover the bodies of Eicke, his adjutant and the pilot.

Meanwhile, news had spread through the division and up the chain of command to Hitler. When Eicke's death was announced to the public on 1 March 1943, Hitler in his eulogy to the man who had given such 'exceptional and unique service to the Reich' announced *Totenkopf*'s 3rd Panzer Grenadier Regiment would be named *Theodor Eicke* in honour of the late *Totenkopf* division's founder and commander. Eicke was given a divisional funeral at the nearby town of Otdochnina on the same day.

Eicke was not a man who was genuinely liked in the SS and Nazi Party. He was too aggressive and headstrong a man for that. However, he was an exceptional and talented organiser and his drive and energy, some felt, would be sorely missed. Perhaps the only place – outside his immediate family – where he was genuinely mourned was his division. *Totenkopf* was Eicke's creation and it was shaped by his personality and beliefs. His iron discipline, utter fanaticism and hatred of the enemy were all transmitted to his soldiers.

In Eicke's view, *Totenkopf* did not retreat and its men waged war with total conviction and ferocity. Yet fanaticism and ferocity do not necessarily make a make a commander as revered by his men as Eicke was. The explanation was relatively simple. He was, to use an appropriate cliché, 'a soldier's general'. While he might have expected absolute courage from his men, Eicke himself shared their hardships. Habitually exposing himself to danger by always being near the front, as his death proved, he expected as much from

Right: Busts of Soviet leaders and artists collected by men of the *Totenkopf* Division as trophies during the battle for Kharkov. Among those shown are Lenin, Marshal Voroshilov and Maxim Gorki.

himself as he did from them. He wore the same clothes, slept in the same bunkers and foxholes, and ate the same rations. Eicke also managed to maintain a remarkable intimacy with his men and in turn they gave him their unquestioning loyalty. It is perhaps a tribute to Eicke and the division he created that it could function perfectly well without him after his death. *Totenkopf* maintained the same reputation for reliability and fought with the same ferocity after its creator's death as it had before.

THE BATTLE OF KHARKOV

Despite the terrible defeat that had just occurred, the Soviet high command pushed an armoured corps south to block the German advance on Kharkov. However, that Soviet corps had fallen into yet another German trap. Hausser deployed *Totenkopf* and *Das Reich* as if he was about to drive upon the city and thus drew the Soviet force onto them while he sent *Leibstandarte* around behind the Soviets. *Totenkopf* and *Das Reich* pushed the Soviet units back northwards toward *Leibstandarte*, which had dug in to block the Soviet retreat. Thus, the hammer of *Totenkopf* and *Das Reich* crushed the last Soviet force blocking the path to Kharkov on the anvil of *Leibstandarte*. With this final obstacle out of the way, on 5 March 1943, *Totenkopf* and *Das Reich* linked up with Hoth's 4th Panzer Army for an offensive to take the city. The ground remained hard and Manstein and Hoth therefore decided to take Kharkov by surrounding it, rather than taking the city itself street by street and thus being sucked into the kind of urban warfare that had proved so costly at Stalingrad.

The vanguard of *Das Reich* reached the western outskirts of Kharkov on 9 March 1943. Had Hausser obeyed his instructions, the SS Panzer Corps would have continued in a sweeping arc around the northern edge of the city to complete its part in Kharkov's encirclement. Hausser, however, could not resist trying

to take the city quickly. He ordered *Das Reich* to halt and prepare to assault the city while he sent *Totenkopf* around the northern edge to block off any Soviet retreat. Then, on 11 March, using *Das Reich* and *Leibstandarte* and one battalion detached from *Totenkopf*, Hausser's men attacked in direct contravention of Hoth's orders. It took three days of vicious street fighting to capture the city and, in Hoth's own estimation, his panzer corps suffered about 11,500

casualties. Meanwhile, *Totenkopf* carried out the plan as envisaged by Hoth and Manstein by completing the encirclement of Kharkov. By 15 March, it had taken the vital bridge crossing the Donetz River at Chuguyev, which trapped any Soviet units trying to flee from Hoth's panzer army. In a defensive battle around the Chuguyev crossings, *Totenkopf* destroyed the elite Soviet 25th Guards Rifle Division as it tried to break out.

Hoth and Manstein had one further goal after the fall of Kharkov, and that was the elimination of the last important Soviet bridgehead over the Donetz at the city of Belgorod. If the Soviets held Belgorod, there remained a considerable threat to the continued German possession of Kharkov, and consequently, on 18 March, the entire panzer corps, *Leibstandarte*, *Das Reich* and *Totenkopf*, drove the final Soviet units out of the city just as the spring thaw began. The thaw

Above: *Totenkopf* officers watch the progress of one of the division's attacks during the battle of Kursk in July 1943. Although the Soviet troops were waiting for them, the division still managed to make good progress.

Left: *Totenkopf* Tigers move forward during the build-up for the Kursk offensive. These massive new tanks had an 88mm gun and thick armour plating, and were used as the spearhead of the *Totenkopf* attack.

turned Russian roads into quagmires and assured, at least for a few weeks, that large-scale operations were impossible. This gave the German divisions a much-needed period of respite.

The victory at Kharkov did much to boost the already high reputation of the SS. Hitler was absolutely delighted. It greatly revived his spirits after the disasters of the winter of 1942–43. His mind turned to even more ambitious plans for the summer and he intended that his crack SS units would do much of the fighting to make these ideas a reality.

OPERATION CITADEL

There were limits to what German resources could achieve in the summer of 1943. Hitler felt that crushing the huge Soviet salient around the town of Kursk that bulged into the German front at the junction of Army Group Centre and Army Group South was a

Right: Panzergrenadiers of II SS Panzer Corps hitch a ride on PzKpfw IIIs during the battle of Kursk. By mid 1943, the PzKpfw III was heavily outclassed on the battlefield, but was still in service as a light tank with *Totenkopf*.

worthwhile target for the summer's operations. Indeed, it was. Destroying the Kursk salient would dramatically shorten the length of the German front; a successful offensive might eliminate up to 15 Soviet armies and capture hundreds of thousands of Soviet prisoners. Success would also release German troops from the front to face the anticipated Allied invasion of southern Europe.

DISSENT

Hitler's generals did not all agree. Two of Germany's most able commanders, Manstein, who headed Army Group South, and Guderian, who was Inspector General of armoured troops, were both set against the attack. Guderian told Hitler on 4 May 1943 'that the attack was pointless; we had only just completed the re-equipment of our eastern front; if we attacked according to the plan … we were certain to suffer heavy tank casualties, which we would not be in a position to replace in 1943'. Manstein was at the same meeting and expressed himself somewhat less forcefully than Guderian. They both believed, however, that Germany's carefully nurtured panzers should be saved and the Soviets should be allowed to go on the offensive. This way the Germans could withdraw gradually, allowing the Soviets to overextend themselves and make a German counterstroke all the more damaging, as had happened at Kharkov. Hitler, however, was determined and insisted that the planning for an offensive against the Kursk salient, codenamed Operation *Zitadelle* (Citadel), be carried forward.

One of the main problems with Hitler's plan was that its advantages were as clear to the Soviet high command as they were to Hitler. Thus, as German preparations on the north and south side of the bulge began, the Soviets also undertook corresponding counter measures. They set about turning the Kursk salient into an impregnable fortress. The Soviets constructed six interlocking defensive belts to a depth of

40km (25 miles), with covering belts of trenches, bunkers, strong points and barbed wire. Supporting these defences in depth were 20,000 guns, a third of which were anti-tank weapons. They laid minefields to a density of 2500 anti-personnel and 2200 anti-tank mines per mile of the front. In total, 400,000 mines were laid. Streams were dammed to create impassable flooded areas. What would otherwise be an area of rich and fertile agricultural land had become a gigantic obstacle course for the Germans. The Soviet high command pressed the local civilian population into digging 4800km (3000miles) of defensive ditches, carefully crisscrossed to allow mobility for Russian infantry. To back up and man these defences, the

Soviets amassed a huge force of aircraft and the largest concentration of tanks ever assembled. The Soviet commanders Vatutin and Rokossovsky crammed seven armies – 1,336,000 men and 3444 tanks – into the Kursk salient. Indeed, 75 per cent of all Soviet armour available to Stavka at that time was in and around the area.

GERMAN DISPOSITIONS

Facing this awesome accumulation of Soviet defensive power to the north of the bulge in the Orel sector was General Walter Model's 9th Army. Model had three panzer and two infantry corps, a total of 19 first-line divisions. On the southern half of the Kursk salient, the German forces were even more formidable. Hermann Hoth's 4th Panzer Army was made up of two panzer corps: the 48th and Paul Hausser's re-designated 2nd SS Panzer Corps. The 52nd Infantry Corps was anchoring the Army's left flank. To the

Below: A *Totenkopf* Tiger tank waits before another attack is launched. The unit's divisional symbol for Kursk – III – is clearly visible on the vertical armour plating on the front left of the tank.

Above: Two *Totenkopf* soldiers at Kursk: Otto Baum (left), commander of the 5th SS Panzergrenadier Regiment *Thule*, and Karl Ullrich, commander of the 3rd Battalion, whose men penetrated furthest into the Soviet defences.

right of Hoth's army was Panzer Group Kempf, made up of the 3rd Panzer and 11th Army Corps. Hoth's force, compressed into a 45-km (28-mile) front, contained some of the finest divisions of the Wehrmacht. The 3rd, 6th, 7th, 11th and 19th Panzer Divisions, the elite armoured division *Grossdeutschland* and the best formations of the *Waffen-SS*, *Leibstandarte* Adolf Hitler, *Das Reich* and *Totenkopf*. This was a total force of around 900,000 soldiers and 2700 tanks.

Hitler had set much store on the new generation of German tanks and armoured vehicles: the Tiger, the Ferdinand and the Panther, even though the Panther was not yet ready. As Guderian pointed out, the Panther upon which everyone was relying so heavily was 'still suffering from the many teething troubles inherent in all new equipment'. Most of the German tanks were the German Army's reliable old workhorse, the PzKpfw IV, and also the lighter PzKpfw III; this was certainly the case in the three *Waffen-SS* divisions. Altogether, they fielded some 422

tanks and assault guns, of which 170 were PzKpfw IVs. In battle, these tanks formed the outer edges of the division's armoured wedge or *Panzerkeil*, centred on the core of Tiger tanks.

Zitadelle opened at 0350 hours on 5 July with simultaneous German assaults from north and south, after amassed artillery barrage. If the Germans expected this barrage to soften Soviet resistance, however, they were wrong. In the north, Model's 9th Army soon became deadlocked in a desperate battle of attrition and only managed to advance a few kilometres into the salient. The Soviets had expected the main weight of the German attack to come from Model's army and had consequently concentrated the bulk of their forces in the northern sector. Thus, none of Model's units penetrated deeper than 16km

(10miles). Their objective, the town of Kursk, was about 80km (50miles) from the German start line.

In fact, the most powerful German thrust came from Hoth's 4th Panzer Army to the south. *Totenkopf* was the wing division on the extreme right flank of Hoth's army. The division had to keep pace with the advance of Hausser's Panzer Corps, but also screen

Left: The results of the carnage at Prokhorovka: two knocked-out Soviet T-34s. The Soviet tanks engaged their German opponents at oblique angles, which stopped the longer-ranged German guns from picking them off at will.

Below: A map showing the events around Kharkov and Kursk in 1943. After the Soviet attack, Manstein's counter recaptured Kharkov. The inset map shows the southern thrust towards Kursk in which *Totenkopf* took part in July.

the flank against any Soviet counterstroke from the east. Opposite the three SS divisions were the mixed armour and infantry of Soviet 1st Tank Army and 69th Army, dug in to formidable defensive works.

HARD STRUGGLE

Within an hour, the three SS divisions were entangled in heavy fighting. Although they made fairly rapid progress over the first minefields, which had been well swept by the SS engineers, *Totenkopf* had to smash its way through 52nd Guards Division. By evening, *Totenkopf*, with its new Panther and Tiger tanks, had reached the Russian second line, and even captured the village of Yakhontovo and taken an important command post of the Soviet 69th Army. *Leibstandarte* and *Das Reich* had done similarly well. They had penetrated about 19km (12miles) into the Russian

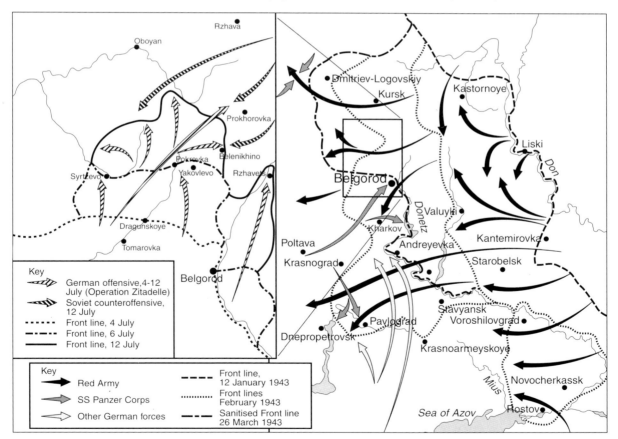

Key
- ⫷⫷⫷ German offensive, 4-12 July (Operation Zitadelle)
- ⫸⫸⫸ Soviet counteroffensive, 12 July
- ·········· Front line, 4 July
- —·—·— Front line, 6 July
- ——— Front line, 12 July

Key
- ➤ Red Army
- ➤ SS Panzer Corps
- ➤ Other German forces
- ——— Front line, 12 January 1943
- ·········· Front lines February 1943
- —— Sanitised Front line 26 March 1943

Right: A *Totenkopf* **8cm GrW 34 mortar team walk past their comrades riding in the Soviet fashion on the back of one of the division's tanks at Kursk. The GrW 34 was a popular infantry support weapon amongst the troops.**

defences. The 2nd SS Panzer Corps made just as good progress the following day and, although *Leibstandarte* and *Das Reich* were entangled in the Soviet defences, *Totenkopf* managed to break free and penetrate 32km (20miles) north. By dusk of 6 July, the division was astride the Belgorod–Kursk railroad.

SS SUCCESS

By 7 July, the advance of the SS Panzer Corps looked most promising. *Totenkopf* had managed to advance some 48km (30miles) into the Russian line, although *Das Reich* and *Leibstandarte* had had a tougher time of it. Given the damage inflicted on the Soviets and the numbers of Soviet prisoners taken, it appeared to the men of the SS Panzer Corps that they were poised on the edge of victory. However, they had not yet even encountered the main Russian opposition. The SS Panzer Corps had advanced considerably faster than its neighbours to the left, a fact which the Soviets took full advantage of, counterattacking against the flank of *Leibstandarte*. *Leibstandarte* was forced to hold back its advance to cover the rear and flank of the advancing SS divisions. Meanwhile, although Hoth and Manstein were keen to release *Totenkopf* from its flank protection task and allow it to continue its advance at a pace, *Totenkopf* was forced to pause throughout 8 July. The division had to wait for 167th Infantry Division to advance and take over its role of guarding the corps' right flank.

With *Totenkopf* relieved, the SS Panzer Corps threw its weight against the last Soviet line and, on 10 July, the division reached the River Psel. That afternoon, the 3rd battalion of the 1st Panzer Grenadier Regiment, commanded by *Standartenführer* Karl Ullrich, cleared the last Soviet defenders from its sector and crossed the river, the last remaining natural barrier between 4th Panzer Army and its objective, Kursk. Ullrich's men established a bridgehead on the north bank, but were forced to wait for the arrival of

heavier bridging equipment. *Totenkopf* and its two fellow *Waffen-SS* divisions mopped up the remaining Soviet resistance in the area throughout 11 July and regrouped in readiness for the delivery of what they thought would be the final and decisive blow.

The success of Hausser's Panzer Corps alarmed the Soviet command considerably. Vatutin therefore drew into his huge reserves and, early on 11 July, he ordered General Nikolai Rotmistrov's 5th Tank Army south to crush Hausser's corps. He was worried enough to request an additional reserve of two tank corps from the neighbouring Steppe front. On the morning of 12 July, the Soviet 5th Guard and 5th Guard Tank Armies clashed with 2nd SS Panzer Corps around the village of Prokhorovka. The Soviets committed a total of seven corps, with more than 850 Soviet tanks and SU-85 assault guns. Wave after wave of T-34s appeared at speed, attacking obliquely to the German line, which deprived the German tanks of the luxury of picking the Russian tanks off at a distance with their more powerful main armament. In this, the largest armoured battle of all time, which raged for eight hours around the orchards and cornfields near Prokhorovka, the battle of Kursk was decided. The official Soviet history of the battle gives an excellent sense of the closeness and confused nature of the engagement:

'It destroyed the enemy's ability to control his leading units and sub-units. The close combat deprived the Tigers of the advantages which their powerful gun and thick armour conferred, and they were successfully shot up at close range by the T-34s. Immense numbers of tanks were mixed up all over the battlefield; there was neither time nor space to disengage and re-form ranks. Fired at short range, shells penetrated front and side armour. There were frequent explosions as ammunition blew up, throwing tank turrets dozens of yards from their stricken vehicles … on the scorched black earth, smashed tanks were blazing like torches. It was difficult to tell who was attacking and who was defending.'

Smoke and dust obscured the fighting and the tanks became so interlocked that it was impossible to

call up artillery or air support. The T-34s, at point-blank range, fired into the sides and rear of the Tigers, Panthers and older PzKpfw IVs and PzKpfw IIIs. The close range negated the advantage which the superior German tank guns on the Panther and the Tiger gave the SS armoured units. When the T-34s ran out of ammunition, the Soviet crews often physically rammed the German tanks. Dismounted T-34 crews then set about destroying German tanks on foot, using grenades and mines.

Totenkopf faced two Soviet corps – the equivalent of four divisions – and was soon forced onto the defensive. Although outnumbered perhaps four to one in both tanks and infantry, the division held throughout the 12th, 13th and into the afternoon of 14 July, to hold the two Soviet corps and prevent any penetration of Hausser's flank. However, it was at a price. When the Soviets called off their attacks on the evening of 14 July, *Totenkopf* had lost more than half its tanks and vehicles, and taken immense casualties. While *Totenkopf* might have been able to protect the panzer corps' flanks successfully, Operation *Zitadelle* as a whole had failed. The fighting of 13–15 July rumbled on, but the Germans knew they had no chance of achieving success. Hitler had his eyes elsewhere, however, and was worried about the new developments in the Mediterranean.

SOUTHERN THREAT

The British and Americans had landed in Sicily on 10 July and Hitler began to believe that in this theatre lay a great danger to Germany. He felt that it required the talents of his elite SS divisions to shore up the Mediterranean because, despite the failure of *Zitadelle*, the *Waffen-SS* had risen even higher in his estimations. The SS Panzer Corps had penetrated deepest into the salient and had not broken under the immense Russian counterattack. Hitler constantly told his generals that he only wished that the rest of

Left: A well-camouflaged *Totenkopf* MG34 machine gun team. The camouflaged face masks with vertical vision slits were used by the *Waffen-SS* to hide the paleness of their faces against a natural background.

the *Wehrmacht* was so reliable. He officially cancelled *Zitadelle* on 13 July so as to free up the SS divisions for transfer to Italy.

Manstein protested, claiming that the removal of these units would inevitably mean that the gains made at Kursk would have to be relinquished and the battle would have been fought in vain. Hitler was adamant so, essentially, the great sacrifices of *Totenkopf* and the rest of the German Army at Kursk achieved nothing. Heinz Guderian summed the battle up thus:

'By the failure of Citadel we had suffered a decisive defeat. The armoured formations, reformed and re-equipped with so much effort, had lost heavily both in men and equipment and would now be unemployable for a long time to come. It was problematical whether they could be rehabilitated in time to defend the Eastern Front; as for being able to use them in defence of the Western Front against the Allied landings that threatened for next spring, this was even more questionable. Needless to say the Russians exploited their victory to the full. There were to be no more periods of quiet on the Eastern Front. From now on the enemy was in undisputed possession of the initiative.'

CHAPTER SIX

END GAME

The failure of the offensive at Kursk marked the beginning of the long retreat back to Germany for the *Wehrmacht*, and *Totenkopf* were called upon to fight continuous rearguard actions against the harrying Soviet forces in an attempt to preserve the army's strength.

At Kursk, *Totenkopf* had lost more than half its vehicles and taken huge casualties. The exhausted and battered division was taken out of the line to recuperate while a few extra tanks and assault guns were found. They came nowhere near to making up the losses that the unit had suffered. Kursk had been the zenith of *Totenkopf*'s offensive power and, like so many other German formations, it would never again possess anything like the strength it had had in the battles of the summer of 1943.

Four days after the abrupt termination of Operation *Zitadele*, Hitler ordered Hausser's SS Panzer Corps to Italy with the intention of checking the forthcoming Allied invasion there. Thus, *Leibstandarte*, *Das Reich* and *Totenkopf* were pulled back to the relative calm and quiet of Kharkov to wait for their trains. The Soviets, however, did not allow the Germans any respite. General Malinovsky launched a counterattack against the Germans in the Donetz basin on 25 July 1943, utilising large and fresh Red Army units. Malinovsky's men overran Field Marshal von Manstein's positions on the Mius River. Thus,

Left: Well wrapped-up in Hungary in early 1945. Hitler decided that Budapest was worth fighting for, and wasted precious resources on attempting to reach the city even after it fell in February.

Hitler detached *Das Reich* and *Totenkopf* from *Leibstandarte* and, along with the 3rd Panzer Corps, made up of 16th and 23rd Panzer Divisions, they were moved south to Stalino, and went into action on 30 July to seal the breach. After three days of fighting, they had blunted Malinovsky's breakthrough and stabilised the front. Hitler still intended to send the three SS divisions to Italy, where Mussolini had just been overthrown and arrested on 25 July. However, the vast Soviet resources available meant that they could launch another pair of offensives straight away and plunge the German front around Kursk into crisis again. Three whole Soviet fronts (comparable to three army groups) attacked on two axes towards Belgorod and Orel. Such a massive assault meant there could be no question of sending all the crack SS divisions to Italy, so *Totenkopf* and *Das Reich* were rushed north to protect Manstein's left flank, while only *Leibstandarte* entrained for the move west.

Using their six-to-one superiority in tanks and guns, the five armies of the two Soviet fronts drove into Hoth's Panzer Army and Army Detachment Kempf, and quickly knocked them from their *Zitadele* start lines where Hitler had ordered them to withdraw to after Kursk. The Red Army breakthrough between 4th Panzer Army and Kempf's forces bypassed Kharkov to the north and then swung

Above: What appear to be two *Totenkopf* Panther tanks on the Eastern Front. *Totenkopf* converted (albeit in name only) to a panzer division in October 1943. It later began to receive the new Panther tanks as replacements.

southwest towards Polotova. Marshal Vatutin's intention was to drive deep into Manstein's rear and cut off Army Group South by capturing the crossings over Dnieper. Manstein recognised the Soviet objectives and ordered *Das Reich* and *Totenkopf* to the west of Kharkov. They were first to prevent the Soviet drive on Dnieper, and then to stop the Soviet tanks wheeling south and surrounding Kharkov, thereby encircling Army Detachment Kempf which, in accordance with Hitler's no-retreat order, had been instructed to stand outside Kharkov. For a week, *Das Reich* and *Totenkopf* held the Soviet armoured spearheads at bay and prevented them reaching the Dnieper. However, Kempf soon recognised that Kharkov could not be held and, on 13 August, issued orders that it be evacuated. Hitler personally countermanded Kempf's instructions, demanding that the city be held at all costs. When this proved a military impossibility, Kempf withdrew on 22 August to escape encirclement and Hitler dismissed the general. Despite

Hitler's order, local *Das Reich* and *Totenkopf* counter-attacks blunted and slowed the Russian advance, thereby allowing German forces to be smoothly withdrawn and subsequently reorganised in the wake of the loss of Kharkov.

'FIRE BRIGADES'

Totenkopf and also *Das Reich*'s performance around Kharkov, despite the mauling they had taken at Kursk, proved that they were still first-class formations. In fact, their role as so-called 'fire brigades', shuttled from one point of crisis to another to dampen down the worst of the Soviet attacks, typified their role for the remainder of the war. Their success in halting the Soviet advance on the Dnieper had given

Manstein time to retreat and re-deploy. The two SS divisions had helped divert a major disaster and given Manstein precious time to reorganise the front. The field marshal recognised that his army group could no longer hold the Donetz Line, and sought to withdraw to the natural defensive barrier of the Dnieper River. He met Hitler a number of times at the end of August and beginning of September 1943, before securing Hitler's permission to withdraw (for once) the 4th Panzer Army and the 8th Army to the river. Manstein detached *Totenkopf* and *Das Reich*, and, together with the elite army division *Grossdeutschland*, they covered the 8th Army's retreat across the Dnieper before retiring to the western bank of the river themselves.

There was no respite. In the first week of October, the Soviets launched an attack against German forces in the great bend of the Dnieper between Kremenchug and Zaporozhye. Then, on 15 October, the new Soviet 2nd Ukrainian Front, with a total of six armies, punched through the German front between the 8th Army and the left wing of General Hube's 1st Panzer Army. The Soviet armoured spearhead, once across to the west of the Dnieper, drove south, straight for Krivoi Rog, the supply and communication centre for Army Group South. Krivoi Rog contained the supply and ammunition dumps for the region, plus a good number of locomotives and rolling stock that were vital for the continued effective functioning of

Below: By 1944 and the Soviet summer offensive, *Totenkopf* was constantly being used to plug holes in the German front line. Each time the Red Army broke through, the division would launch a counter-attack.

Army Group South. Manstein could not allow this to be lost and he threw what reserves he could find into the path of the Soviet advance, while scraping together enough armour to launch a decent counterattack. He managed to find six weakened armoured divisions, including SS *Totenkopf*, which that October had been designated a panzer division, with the title 3rd SS Panzer Division *Totenkopf*. However, this did not mean that *Totenkopf* received any great influx of fresh armour and men. On 27 October, *Totenkopf*, now commanded by Hermann Priess, the division's

old artillery regiment commander, led 40th Panzer Corps (also including 14th and 24th Panzer Divisions) into the right flank of the Soviet advance. The counter-thrust broke up two Soviet armoured corps and nine rifle divisions. The Soviets lost more than 300 tanks and 5000 prisoners, and staggered back half the distance to the Dnieper, again allowing Manstein, albeit temporarily, to stabilise the front.

Holding Krivoi Rog was vital to the maintenance of Army Group South's position, particular-

armoured assaults. The battle raged for three days between 18 and 21 November, during which *Totenkopf* claimed to have destroyed 247 Soviet tanks. The Soviets did not pause for long and came at *Totenkopf* again on 25 November and, for three days and nights, the division endured further constant Soviet attacks.

Although, as already stated, *Totenkopf* never regained the strength it possessed before Kursk, as a favoured SS division it received more replacements in men and equipment than most. Part of its success in these defensive battles around the Dnieper can be put down to it being considerably stronger than many of the divisions around it. As of 22 November, *Totenkopf* contained three full battalions of panzer grenadiers, one weak (40 per cent of establishment) battalion of tanks, 75 per cent of its artillery, 75 per cent of its flak, 55 per cent of its engineer battalion and nearly full-strength supply and support units.

FRESH SOVIET ATTACK

It was a good job too, because, on 5 December 1943, the Soviets renewed their offensive, crushed what was left of 384th Division and overpowered the 1st Panzer Army's left flank. The following day, the Russian flanks broke into open country and threatened to envelop Krivoi Rog from the northwest. Hube ordered *Totenkopf* into the crisis sector and, true to form, the division checked the Soviet advance. Hube then scraped together his best armoured forces – *Totenkopf* and the 11th and 13th Panzer Divisions – and launched a major counterattack on 19 December, which stopped the Russians and restored the front, leaving Krivoi Rog in German hands. The city eventually fell at the end of February 1944, but the desperate defence of *Totenkopf* and its fellow divisions had bought the Germans enough time to remove the bulk of the supplies, ammunition, vehicles and rolling stock that would have been lost had the Soviet thrust reached Krivoi Rog sooner.

ly as Hitler insisted that the army group retain its position in the Crimea. Had the Russians taken this crucial rail junction, the German 17th Army would have been cut off in the Crimean peninsula. The Soviets realised this and continued to build up forces to the northeast and, on 14 November, attacked the weakest point in Hube's 1st Panzer Army, the sector held by 384th Infantry Division. Hube sent *Totenkopf* to seal the gap. On 15 November, the division counterattacked and halted the advance. They dug in and waited for the inevitable massive Soviet

Totenkopf, however, was long gone from the sector by that time.

Manstein ordered the division north with the elite and still-powerful *Grossdeutschland* Division to the area of Kirovograd to deliver a fierce counteroffensive blow to Soviets in the area, allowing the German 8th Army to pull back safely. The winter and spring of 1944 was characterised by a series of constant withdrawals from one natural barrier to another in the face of constant and massive Soviet offensives, which pushed the Germans back towards the western borders of the Soviet Union. General Wöhler, commanding the 8th Army, again chose *Totenkopf* to act as rearguard, as the army withdrew to new positions on the Bug River. This time, however, Soviet strength was such that *Totenkopf* and the rest of the rearguard could not slow the advance enough, and the 8th

Above: To compensate for losses and permanently below-strength units, *Waffen-SS* soldiers were increasingly given greater firepower. The MG42 machine gun was capable of a cyclic rate of fire of up to 1550 rounds per minute.

Army position on the Bug soon collapsed. Indeed, in the first of week of March, the whole of Army Group South fell back on the river Dniester, the border between Romania and the Soviet Union. Yet again, the German position could not hold in the face of the converging 1st Ukrainian Front of Marshal Malinovsky and the 2nd Ukrainian Front of General Tolbukhin. They crossed the Dniester in early April 1944 and pushed into Romania. Once again, *Totenkopf* acted, along with the 47th Panzer Corps, as an armoured rearguard, protecting the withdrawal of the 6th Army through Romania, which took them to the foothills of the Carpathian Mountains where *Totenkopf* dug in on 1 May in anticipation of a fresh Soviet attack.

NEW COMMANDER

Thankfully for the division, that assault did not occur for the time being. The Soviet spring offensive had petered out in the deep mud of the spring thaw. Throughout May and June 1944, there was a lull in Romania. Himmler managed to find considerable reinforcements for the division and new consignments of artillery tanks and guns. Hermann Priess was transferred to the command of *Das Reich* in May and was replaced by Hellmuth Becker, who had served in the division for some time. Wöhler pulled the division out of the line and allow it to refit in reserve. However, the Army High Command was eager to get its hands on such a powerful and reliable division as *Totenkopf*. Hitler reckoned that the Soviet summer offensive would be directed against the southern flank of Army Group Centre and drive northwards

towards Army Group North. Thus, the Army High Command began shifting forces northwards to Army Group Centre and Army Group North. On 23 June 1944, the Soviets launched Operation Bagration against Army Group Centre, committing 2.4 million men, 5200 tanks and 5300 aircraft in the largest offensive of the war so far, on a 320-km (200-mile) front. In the three weeks that followed, Army Group Centre lost 28 divisions and about 350,000 men, as the Soviets drove towards Poland and East Prussia.

Unsurprisingly, *Totenkopf* was ordered north on 25 June to join the 4th Army. However, as Army Group Centre disintegrated, *Totenkopf* became ensnarled in the rail bottleneck to Army Group Centre's west. The last units of the division detrained in eastern Poland on 7 July. Hitler had given command of what was left

Below: Elements of the 4th SS Panzer Corps retreating through Hungary in the spring of 1945 in the face of the Soviet advance. A motorised column including a halftrack towing a 7.5cm Pak 40 gun passes dug-in infantry.

of Army Group Centre to Field Marshal Model. To buy time, Model sent *Totenkopf* to the city of Grodno, to hold the right flank of the 4th Army in the north and the left wing of the 2nd Army in the south. For 11 days, outnumbered seven to one in troops and ten to one in tanks, *Totenkopf* held on. However, *Totenkopf* could only slow, not stop, the Russian offensive and, on 18 July, Model gave the division permission to abandon Grodno and withdraw west in the retreat towards Warsaw.

The Red Army had now driven deep into Poland and *Totenkopf*, along with the armoured Paratroop Division led by Hermann Göring, held the city of

Siedlce 80km (50miles) east of Warsaw for four days, in the face of the Soviet 2nd Tank Army. Their resistance allowed the German 2nd Army to retreat to the Vistula River. On 28 July, they abandoned the town and withdrew towards Warsaw. The two divisions slowed the Soviet advance on Warsaw over the next eight days and allowed Model to reorganise a defence along the river. The Soviets had advanced 725km (450miles) in just over a month and had reached the end of their tether in supply terms. The offensive ground to a halt on the Vistula in early August. This slowing and eventual stop were aided by some fierce counterattacks from Model. With the Red Army so

Left: Assault guns of the 4th SS Panzer Corps move forward for yet another wasteful attack on Soviet forces defending Budapest. The assault guns' low profile and thick armour made them formidable opponents.

near, the Polish home army rose against the German occupation of Warsaw. The revolt was suppressed with almost indescribable brutality by units of the *Waffen-SS* (although none from *Totenkopf*) and the notorious Dirlewanger and Kaminski brigades of SS irregulars. Their behaviour was so shocking that Colonel General Guderian and *SS-Gruppenführer* Fegelein, the SS liaison officer at Hitler's headquarters, had the units withdrawn.

Using the brief lull, Model reorganised the German defence. *Totenkopf* and the 5th SS Panzer Division *Wiking* formed the 4th Panzer Corps commanded by *SS-Gruppenführer* Herbert Gille and Model placed this corps some 48km (30miles) northeast of Warsaw, where he expected the renewal of the Soviet offensive. The Soviets attacked on 14 August and, for a week, the well–dug-in SS divisions repulsed a combined enemy force of 15 rifle divisions and two armoured brigades. The Soviets regrouped on 21 August and resumed their assault four days later, the weight of their attack falling on *Totenkopf*. On 26 August, eight rifle divisions and a motorised rifle brigade with air support finally dislodged Becker's division from its positions and the entire Panzer Corps was driven back west towards Warsaw. On 11 September, *Totenkopf* temporarily drove the Soviet vanguard out of the suburbs of northeastern Warsaw, where the division managed to hold until the Soviet offensive petered out 10 days later.

There followed a three-week lull until 10 October, when yet another Soviet offensive forced the 4th Panzer Corps to withdraw 32km (20miles) westwards. The front stabilised as the Soviets failed to penetrate the SS divisions and the Soviets abandoned their assault on 27 October. Calm returned to the front around Warsaw. *Totenkopf*'s performance in these defensive battles against the Soviets had not escaped Hitler's attention and he remarked that he wished he had a few extra battalions to send the division as

'whenever one sent them reinforcement [they] always counterattack[ed] successfully'.

While the position in Poland might have stabilised, the rest of the German situation in Europe did not look good. The British and Americans had landed successfully in Normandy in June and, by the autumn, were on the western frontier of Germany. In Italy, the British and American armies there were relentlessly pushing the Germans back northwards. Rome had recently fallen. In the Balkans, a Soviet offensive that summer and autumn had overrun all of Romania and Bulgaria, and this had forced the Germans to abandon Greece and retreat through Yugoslavia to Hungary.

The situation changed briefly in December when Hitler attempted to regain the upper hand in the west by launching the Ardennes offensive. He aimed to split the Allied armies in half and recapture Antwerp, the Allies' most vital supply port. Utilising precious German armour reserves, including the newly created 6th SS Panzer Army of four SS panzer divisions under Sepp Dietrich, the attack was launched on 16 December 1944. Although there were some initial successes, American resistance stiffened and held. The failure in the Ardennes ended all hope of victory in the west (not that anyone other than Hitler believed that was possible anyway) and destroyed vital quantities of what limited armour and fuel the Germans had left.

BUDAPEST

In Hungary, the situation was no better. In October 1944, it was clear to the Germans that the Hungarian head of state, Admiral Horthy, was about to abandon his German allies and attempt to negotiate terms with the Soviets. Thus, *SS-Obersturmbannführer* Otto Skorzeny led a spectacular coup against the Horthy government. A pro-German puppet regime was installed. This did not halt the Soviet advance into Hungary, however, and the Red Army drove to the Danube south of Budapest and established bridgeheads on the west bank. The Germans had set up strong defensive positions around Lake Balaton southwest of Budapest and, for a time, the Soviet

advance was temporarily slowed. Nonetheless, on 24 December, the Soviets had managed to encircle Budapest, garrisoned by the remnants of 8th SS Cavalry Division *Florian Geyer*, 22nd SS Volunteer Cavalry Division *Maria Theresia* and 18th SS Volunteer Panzer Grenadier Division *Horst Wessel*.

Even as the Ardennes offensive failed, Hitler's thoughts were turning to the possibility of another offensive, an assault that would reverse the ever-worsening situation in the east. To the horror of his generals, who wanted to preserve what limited resources in manpower and armour that Germany still had for the defensive battles in Germany proper, Hitler turned his attention to Hungary and, more

Above: Massed T-34/85s accompanied by Soviet infantry launch a counterattack on 4th SS Panzer Corps during the latter's attempt to relieve Budapest. *Totenkopf* were forced to pull back by overwhelming Soviet forces.

specifically, Budapest. Hitler decided that Budapest must be relieved and he turned to what he considered to be amongst his most reliable forces: *Totenkopf* and *Wiking*. At Hitler's personal order, *SS-Gruppenführer* Herbert Gille's 4th SS Panzer Corps was selected to lead the assault on the Hungarian capital. *Totenkopf* and *Wiking* were pulled out of the line west of Warsaw and sent by train via Prague, Vienna and Bratislava to western Hungary, where they moved to jumping-off points ready for the drive on Budapest.

Totenkopf and *Wiking* launched their attack towards Budapest on New Year's Day 1945. They did not get very far. The advance stalled a few miles forward in face of the resistance of the Soviet 4th Guard Army and 6th Guard Tank Army. For the next 10 days, the two SS divisions ground on at the pace of about a mile a day but, by 11 January, fierce Soviet counterattacks had stopped 4th SS Panzer Corps and forced it onto the defensive. Despite this failure, Hitler was determined that Budapest be recaptured and, on 8 January, he ordered Sepp Dietrich's 6th SS Panzer Army to be moved from the Western Front to Hungary. In the meantime, he ordered the exhausted 4th SS Panzer Corps to attack towards Budapest again, without waiting for Dietrich. The second attack began on 18 January and resulted in quite remarkable progress. By the following day, *Totenkopf* and *Wiking* had advanced 65km (40miles) and captured the town of Dunapentele on the Danube. The success was only temporary, however, and, on the following day, resistance stiffened and held. In the meantime, the Soviets assembled the 26th and 46th Armies and counterattacked on 27 January. This drove 4th SS Panzer Corps back in confusion, although they soon managed to re-establish themselves in the Bakony Forest north of Lake Balaton. In these dense woods, *Totenkopf* dug in and awaited the arrival of 6th SS Panzer Army.

OPERATION SPRING AWAKENING

Dietrich's last panzer divisions reached Hungary at the beginning of March 1945. The offensive, code-named Spring Awakening (*Frühlingserwachen*), was to drive the Soviets from the last oilfields in German possession around Lake Balaton, knock them back across the Danube and retake Budapest, which had finally fallen on 11 February. Only 790 men of the 70,000-strong garrison managed to fight their way back to German lines. The Soviets predicted exactly where the major offensive would be and therefore strengthened their defences in this area. The offensive opened on 6 March in heavy snow. Despite the

appalling conditions, the *Waffen-SS* threw themselves into the battle with their customary determination and élan. However, they ran into trouble almost immediately. Nonetheless, their ferocity and professionalism – despite the fact that these SS divisions were a pale shadow of what they had been two years earlier – meant that they pierced the Russian lines in various places. Dietrich's command, including 4th SS Panzer Corps and *Totenkopf*, had, by 9 March, advanced an average of 32km (20miles) from their starting line.

On 13 March, the offensive was halted due to Soviet resistance and the thaw that turned the roads and surrounding countryside into a quagmire. On 16 March, Marshal Tolbukhin's 3rd Ukrainian Front shifted to the offensive against the exhausted 6th SS Panzer Army. The 9th Guard Tank Army smashed into the *Totenkopf* division, overwhelmed them and drove into the rear of the 4th SS Panzer Corps. The *Wiking* division, now under the command of *Totenkopf* veteran Karl Ullrich, was surrounded and, disobeying Hitler's orders to stand fast, broke out westwards. Despite Hitler's hysterical demands that the 6th SS Panzer Army remain in place, Dietrich, too, authorised a general retreat towards the Austrian frontier. Hitler was livid with rage and sent the following message to Dietrich: 'The Führer believes that the troops have not fought as the situation demanded and orders that the SS divisions *Leibstandarte*, *Das Reich*, *Totenkopf* and *Hohenstaufen* be stripped of their armbands.' It was an insult that cut deeply into the SS, who valued their insignia and, while Dietrich was saddened and inclined to forgive Hitler, most of the soldiers were not. According to legend, Joachim Peiper, a highly-decorated veteran of *Leibstandarte* who had fought at Kursk and the battle of the Bulge, suggested that his men gather all their combat decorations in a chamber pot and send it to Hitler.

What was left of *Totenkopf* withdrew up the main road up to Bratislava and Vienna, with the remnants of 6th SS Panzer Army. On 3 April, *Totenkopf* halted in the southern suburbs of Vienna and, with the rest of what once had been elite SS divisions, put up largely symbolic resistance to the two Soviet fronts converging

on the city. Dr Lother Rendulic had received command of Army Group South and had been ordered that Vienna should be held at all costs; however, he does not seem to have countermanded Dietrich's withdrawal from Vienna to the west. On 13 April, the Soviets captured the city.

Meanwhile, the 3rd US Army was driving towards Regensburg, threatening the rear of Army Group South's position. At about this time, the Army High Command ordered the following: 'It is decisive for the fate of the Reich that the eastern front be held. The Americans, however, are to be offered delaying resistance for the sake of honour.' As the Russian offensive shifted away from the 6th SS Panzer Army, ammunition was down to two days and food eight days supply and, as Rendulic noted, 'a continuation of fighting was

Above: The ruins of Budapest after its liberation by the Soviets. 'Spring Awakening' was the last significant German offensive of the war, and virtually destroyed a number of the best SS divisions, including *Totenkopf*.

unthinkable'. The Americans were not even offered delaying resistance. Hellmuth Becker, the last commander of *Totenkopf*, took his surviving units to Lintz.

HITLER DEAD

Hitler had committed suicide on 30 April 1945, but fighting had continued in Berlin until 2 May. The Germans surrendered to British Commander Field Marshal Montgomery in the north and west on 4 May; the Western Allies Supreme Commander accepted the surrender of Germany at Rheims on 7 May.

Finally, the act of surrender was repeated in the presence of representatives of the Soviet Union on 8 May and became effective universally the following day. Becker tried to surrender *Totenkopf* to the 3rd US Army, which accepted this as long as the division disarmed the concentration camp guards at Mauthausen. This Becker's men did, before turning themselves over to the Americans. They were promptly handed over to the Soviets. Immediately after their seizure, they were transported to detention camps and, if they survived, spent many years in Soviet labour camps. It is appropriate to end with a quota-

tion about their treatment by the Soviets from Charles Sydnor: 'as a consequence, Becker and most of his officers and many of the men left in *Totenkopf* division suffered a fate grimmer even than their long ordeal in the Russian war'.

Totenkopf fought with ferocity and tenacity over five years and achieved a staggering record of success in combat, whether in the attack or defence. One can but only admire their bravery and ability as soldiers. Clearly they were not just 'soldiers like any others'. There was a willingness to fight on long after most comparable formations would have surrendered or broken and run – as they demonstrated repeatedly on the Eastern Front – and this ability put them amongst the most formidable divisions to fight in World War II. However, this bravery was not merely a product of their soldierly virtues. *Totenkopf* embodied a pure and

Below: Echoing their attempts to relieve Budapest in January 1945, in March *Totenkopf* took part in Operation Spring Awakening as part of the 6th SS Panzer Army. When this failed, the division retreated towards Vienna.

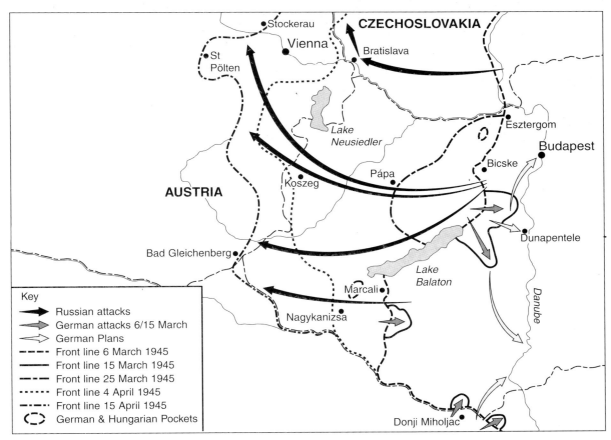

Above: *Totenkopfverbände* personnel on a balcony during rollcall at Mauthausen concentration camp. *Totenkopf*'s last act as a unit was to disarm the camp guards at Mauthausen on behalf of the US 3rd Army.

Left: Adolf Hitler, the man for whom members of the *Totenkopf* had fought and died for five years. After Spring Awakening failed, he repaid them for their faithful service by ordering that they be stripped of their insignia.

political form of National Socialism, the national socialism of Theodor Eicke.

Eicke was a true believer in National Socialism. He instilled his division with a fanatical hatred of its enemies, particularly the Russians. He believed polit-

ical indoctrination was as important as military training. *Totenkopf*'s ability to endure must in part come down to the men's faith in their cause and their commander. Eicke was also certain that they had to be hard, that the division's personnel should be inured to pity. This was particularly evident in the original division, created as it was from the *Totenkopfverbände* of the concentration camp system. Given this political indoctrination and atmosphere of brutality, it is hardly surprising – though not forgivable – that *Totenkopf* and many of its officers in their subsequent SS careers were guilty of some of the most heinous crimes of World War II. Their military achievements must therefore always be viewed in the light of this manifestation of National Socialist evil.

CHAPTER SEVEN

KEY FIGURES

Although the *Totenkopf* Division was almost entirely the product of one man, Theodor Eicke, there were a number of important individuals who were members of the division and played a significant part in its development and performance, both before and after Eicke's death.

The 3rd SS Division *Totenkopf* was built, shaped and led by Theodor Eicke. He formed the first Death's Head Units – the *Totenkopfverbände* – to guard and administer Nazi Germany's concentration camp system, where his rigorous and brutal training regime hardened *Totenkopf* personnel. Eicke was the driving force behind *Totenkopf*'s formation as a *Waffen-SS* division; he trained its personnel, organised its equipment and commanded it in battle. Both *Totenkopf*'s ferocious performance in battle and the atrocities committed by its men can be traced back to Eicke's influence over the division. *Totenkopf* was Theodor Eicke's creation.

THEODOR EICKE (1892–1943)

Eicke was born on 17 October 1892 in Hüdingen in the then-German province of Alsace-Lorraine. He came from a lower middle-class background, similar to that of many leading Nazis, including Hitler. His father, Heinrich Eicke, was stationmaster at the railway station of the Alsatian town of Hampont. The eleventh child of a substantial family, Eicke did not do

Left: *SS-Hauptsturmführer* **(Captain) Max Seela. Seela's squad of *Totenkopf* engineers destroyed seven T-34s on 26 September 1941 near Demyansk on the Eastern Front, winning Seela the Iron Cross.**

well at school and left before matriculating in 1909. He joined the Imperial German Army at the age of 17 and served in the 23rd Infantry Regiment at Landau in the Rhineland-Palatine as a clerk and paymaster. He continued in this role with the 3rd and 22nd Bavarian Infantry regiments during World War I. He won the Iron Cross, Second Class, in 1914.

In 1919, Eicke resigned from the army and found himself pitched into the chaos of postwar Germany. His savings disappeared as inflation ran rampant. To support his wife, Bertha, whom he married in 1914, and his two children – Irma, born 1916, and Herman, born 1920 – he began to work as a police informer. His subsequent career as a police officer, which he pursued in four different towns, ended in dismissal each time for engaging in political agitation against the government, for which he possessed an uncompromising hatred. In 1923, Eicke finally found stable employment with I.G. Faben in Ludwigshafen, first as a salesman, and then as a security officer. He remained with the firm until he entered the SS full time in 1932.

Eicke viewed the postwar German Weimar Republic with considerable distaste and therefore naturally gravitated towards the Nazi Party, which professed similar views towards the German Government and the World War I peace settlement. On 1 December

1928, Theodor Eicke joined the NSDAP with Party Card No. 114-901, and simultaneously joined the ranks of the Ludwigshafen Sturmabteilungen (SA). He transferred to the better-organised SS on 20 August 1930. Eicke believed that there were greater opportunities for advancement within the smaller SS and his rapid rise through the ranks of the organisation proved him right. On 27 November 1930, Heinrich Himmler, *SS-Reichsführer*, appointed him to the rank of *SS-Sturmführer* (second lieutenant) and made him commander of *Sturm* (platoon) No. 148 at Ludwigshafen. Such were Eicke's abilities that Himmler promoted him to *SS-Sturmbannführer* (major) after only three months. His new task was to create a second battalion for the 10th SS Regiment that Himmler intended to establish in the Rhineland-Palatinate area. By the summer of 1931, Eicke had completed his task and once again Himmler rewarded his drive and efficiency with another promotion to *SS-Standartenführer* and command of the newly-formed 10th SS Regiment.

The effect of the worldwide economic depression and the fact that Eicke devoted so much of his time to the SS resulted in him losing his job at I.G. Faben. Unsurprisingly, Eicke put all his energies into the SS and broadened his field of activities to include terrorism. On 6 March 1932, he was arrested and jailed for possession of explosives and for conspiring to carry out a bombing and assassination campaign in Bavaria. He was sentenced to two years in prison, but the sympathetic justice minister Franz Gürtner allowed Eicke temporary parole to 'regain his health'.

EICKE EXILED

Eicke returned to Ludwigshafen and political activism. He soon attracted the attention of the police again and was forced into hiding. Himmler decided that it was now time to spirit Eicke out of trouble and

Left: *SS-Obergruppenführer* **Theodor Eicke, the man who built, shaped and led the** *Totenkopf* **Division until his death on the Eastern Front in 1943. After his death, one of the unit's panzer grenadier regiments was named after him.**

ordered him into Italy. He arrived on 18 September 1932, complete with disguise and false papers. To ease the embarrassment of being forced to flee, Himmler promoted Eicke to *SS-Oberführer* and gave him command of the camp for fugitive SS members based at Malcesine on Lake Garda. Meanwhile, taking advantage of Eicke's absence, the Nazi *gauleiter* of the Palatinate, Josef Bürckel, tried to undermine Eicke's control of the 10th SS Regiment. Eicke fired off a series of letters to his allies in Ludwigshafen threatening use of 'old methods', by which he implied the use of bombs to blow up 'that swine' Bürckel.

Hitler's accession to power on 30 January 1933 changed everything; Eicke was able to return from exile. He promised Himmler that he would not renew his quarrel with Bürckel. This was a promise he promptly forgot on his return to Ludwigshafen. Eicke and a number of his SS comrades staged an armed putsch against his rival, whom they locked in the caretaker's cupboard at the Ludwigshafen Gau Headquarters, which they had seized. Eicke and his colleagues were soon arrested, however, and forced to release Bürckel.

Bürckel had Eicke arrested and branded 'mentally ill and a danger to the community', and he was incarcerated at the Nervenklinik. The *SS-Reichsführer* was so angry that he had Eicke's name struck from the service list of the SS and agreed to his indefinite detention in the hospital. Given the position in which Eicke now found himself, it is a tribute to his considerable drive and abilities that he managed to restart his career and subsequently rise to a position of importance in the SS.

Eicke's psychiatrist, Dr Werner Heyde, did not believe that Eicke was mad and wrote to Himmler stating that he felt his patient was neither disturbed nor a chronic troublemaker. Eicke also pleaded with the *SS-Reichsführer* to reverse his decision. It is perhaps indicative of how the Third Reich worked that, when Himmler relented and had Eicke released from a psychiatric clinic on 26 June 1933, he immediately appointed Eicke commander of the new concentration camp at Dachau.

As noted in the first chapter, Eicke proved a particularly successful concentration camp commandant; his organisation of the SS camp guards and his code of discipline and punishment for the inmates became the model for the entire system. His career was further boosted by his involvement in the Night of the Long Knives in June 1934. Himmler trusted Eicke so completely that the Dachau commandant was given the responsibility of murdering the leader of the SA, Ernst Röhm, at Stadelheim Prison in Munich. Eicke was promoted again, to *SS-Gruppenführer* (lieutenant general), in the wake of the purge, and

made Inspector of Concentration Camps. He had responsibility for the administration of the entire concentration camp system and, within the SS, was responsible only to Himmler. During this period, he also expanded the size of the concentration camp guard units, the so-called *Totenkopfverbände*, or Death's Head Units.

HEYDRICH'S EMNITY

Eicke's drive coupled with his irascibility made him plenty of enemies, some of them very powerful. Eicke had a propensity to carry on inadvisable feuds, as his

Left: Eicke at the *Wolfschanze* (the Wolf's Lair, Hitler's headquarters in East Prussia) in April 1942 after receiving his Oak Leaves to the Knight's Cross from Hitler himself. On Eicke's left is Field Marshal Keitel.

Below: New arrivals at Birkenau extermination camp in 1944 are inspected by the camp guards. *Totenkopf* Division personnel were occasionally rotated back to the concentration camp system.

tussle with Bürckel in Ludwighafen showed. By far the most important enemy he made was Reinhard Heydrich. Heydrich, the talented protégé of the *SS-Reichsführer*, had risen even faster through the ranks of the SS than Eicke. As Charles Sydnor notes: 'Heydrich was the most cynical, ruthless, and feared of the important SS figures; in the jungle of constant and shifting struggles among Himmler's subordinates, confronting Heydrich required considerable skill and courage.'

Their quarrel dated from Eicke's appointment as commandant of Dachau. Heydrich was then chief of the Bavarian police and he had attempted to take over control of the camp, but Eicke's arrival thwarted this ambition. The two men took an instant dislike to each other and Heydrich continuously attempted to undermine Eicke's authority and damage his career. To this end, Heydrich often spread derogatory rumours about Eicke. For example, in 1936, Eicke claimed that Heydrich's subordinates were advocating that the Gestapo (*Geheime Stätspolizei* – Secret State Police) take over the camps and the SS guard units be

Left: *SS-Obersturmführer* Erwin Meierdrees won the Iron Cross for his bravery in the Demyansk encirclement. This picture was taken whilst he was still recovering in hospital in Germany. He was killed in Hungary on 4 January 1945.

Right: Heinz Lammerding, who served with *Totenkopf* in France and for much of the Soviet campaign, briefly leading it in 1943. The atrocities caused by *Das Reich* in France in 1944 took place while he was the division's commander.

removed from Eicke's control because the concentration camps were run by 'a bunch of swine'. Eicke could mitigate this rumour campaign somewhat through his constant access to Himmler. Furthermore, such were the techniques of divide and rule practised within the higher echelons of the Nazi state that Himmler would never allow his ruthless and power-hungry protégé Heydrich to control the massively important concentration camp system.

Indeed, Eicke, who possessed similar cunning to Heydrich and was not scared to stand up to him, provided a useful brake on Heydrich's ambitions for Himmler. Sydnor recounts with some irony the telegrams and condolences received after Eicke's death in 1943 (Heydrich had been assassinated by Czech agents in Prague the previous year). Chief of SS anti-partisan operations, *SS-Obergruppenführer* Erich von dem Bach-Zelewski, declared that Heydrich and Eicke would live on together as guiding spirits of the SS, rather ignoring the fact that in life they loathed each other with some passion.

In the last years of peace before World War II, Eicke had put considerable efforts into expanding and reorganising the *Totenkopfverbände*. By the time war broke out in September 1939, Eicke commanded just over 22,000 men in five regiments of *Totenkopf* (Death's Head) troops, which he had fashioned into a first-class and well-disciplined paramilitary unit. All five regiments operated behind German lines in Poland as independent *Einsatzgruppen* (action groups), with the task of 'pacifying' the Polish population. Eicke did not accompany them into the field, but commanded them from Hitler's special headquarters in his role as *Höhere SS und Polizei Führer*, or

HSSPF (Higher SS and Police Leader). Given their background and training, the *Totenkopf* units acted with unsurprising barbarity in Poland. Nonetheless, Eicke managed to have the *Totenkopf* formations established as a regular SS motorised division in October 1939. He commanded the new division during the French campaign, where it performed well, but also carried out a number of atrocities against British and French troops.

OPERATION BARBAROSSA

After a period of occupation duties, Eicke again led the division during Operation Barbarossa, the invasion of the Soviet Union, in 1941. The *Totenkopf* Division once more made a good showing in the drive towards Leningrad. Eicke was wounded when his command car ran over a mine on 6 July 1941. He

Right: Theodor Eicke (centre) with Max Simon on his left and other *Totenkopf* officers in a bunker during the division's celebration of Christmas in 1941. In the New Year the division would face a massive Soviet counterattack.

returned to the division on 21 September, just as *Totenkopf* faced a massive Russian counterattack. Eicke's division continued to endure the worst that the Soviets could throw at them. Much of the division was cut off in the Demyansk pocket where the unit was virtually destroyed. Despite that, *Totenkopf* refused to give ground or surrender. In recognition of the performance of the *Totenkopf* division, Hitler awarded Eicke the *Ritterkreuz* (the Knight's Cross). In addition, he was honoured with the Oak Leaves to his Knight's Cross on 20 April 1942 and promoted to *SS-Obergruppenführer* (general). Eicke was forced to rebuild the division, as it had sustained massive losses. Between 1 November 1942 and the end of January 1943, Eicke rebuilt the *Totenkopf* division as a Panzer Grenadier formation. It was then sent into the Ukraine, where Eicke died after his plane was shot down on the afternoon of 26 February 1943. His body was recovered by troops of his division at the cost of several lives. Eicke received a divisional funeral near Orelka in the Ukraine.

The SS *Totenkopf* Division was utterly shaped by the character of Theodor Eicke. He brought the same energy, fanaticism and rigid discipline with which he had run the concentration camp system to his command of a *Waffen-SS* division. Essentially, although initially rather limited in his tactical expertise, his determination and utter ruthlessness brought *Totenkopf* results on the battlefield. By the last year of his life, Eicke had gained moderate competency as a divisional commander. What he lacked in formal military training, he made up for through personal energy and effort. He also had the ability to remain calm under intense pressure.

Eicke demanded absolute loyalty from his officers and men, and received it unconditionally. The reason he was so trusted by his troops was that he was very much a soldier's general. He led from the front and was usually found near the hardest fighting. To set an example, he endured the same conditions as his men. During the Demyansk encirclement, Eicke survived on the same rations, wore the same clothes and slept in the same trenches as his infantrymen. To quote Charles Sydnor again: '... the only crime in war Eicke

recognised was cowardice, and his severity in punishing officer and enlisted man alike for this weakness was balanced by a disarming personal intimacy with the proven SS officer and the combat-hardened *Totenkopf* private. As a result, the *Totenkopf* division evinced an extraordinary élan in both victory and defeat and Eicke commanded a near religious devotion from his men who both feared and revered him.'

It is a measure of the indelible stamp that Theodor Eicke left on his division that *Totenkopf* was

Right: Hermann Priess, an artilleryman who rose to command the *Totenkopf* Division from October 1943 to June 1944. He was commander of the *Leibstandarte* Adolf Hitler Division during the Ardennes offensive.

able to endure his loss and maintain its fighting reputation to the end of the war.

MATTHIAS KLEINHEISTERKAMP (1893–1945)

Matthias Kleinheisterkamp had a distinguished career in World War I and won both the First and Second Class of the Iron Cross. After the war, he remained in the army until 1934, when he joined the SS. Given his military background, he naturally transferred to the *SS-Verfügstruppe* in 1938 and was appointed to the SS Führer Schule Braunschweig as an infantry instructor. After a year, Paul Hausser's inspectorate of *Verfügstruppe*, which administered and ran the military training of the armed SS, recruited him. In December 1938, he became commander of the *SS-VT Standarten Deutschland*.

In June 1940, Kleinheisterkamp was personally appointed commander of *Totenkopf*'s 3rd Infantry Regiment at the express wishes of Heinrich Himmler. This immediately placed him on bad terms with Eicke, who resented Kleinheisterkamp's imposition on *Totenkopf*. Eicke had a habit of disciplining senior officers in the same manner as privates, and this brought Eicke into further conflict with Himmler when he confined Kleinheisterkamp to quarters for allegedly failing to carry out an order. Nonetheless, Kleinheisterkamp was competent enough a soldier to replace Eicke until a more senior replacement could be found from 7–18 July 1941 when Eicke was injured by a land mine. Eicke was still keen to get rid of the 3rd Infantry Regiment's commander and, on 27 October 1941, he sent Kleinheisterkamp home on indefinite leave.

According to Eicke, the bitter fighting had destroyed Kleinheisterkamp's nerves and he needed rest to recover. However, Eicke's reasons were probably personal since he had long disliked his subordinate. Again, this action brought Eicke into conflict with Himmler, as it violated the standing order forbidding

the transfer of any senior unit commander without Himmler's approval. Himmler reprimanded Eicke strongly and accused him of disobeying orders out of spite. As for Kleinheisterkamp, his feud with Eicke did nothing to hamper his later career; he was transferred to command the SS *Das Reich* Division, where he was awarded the Knight's Cross. He later held various senior positions, ending the war commanding the 11th SS Army Corps.

GEORG KEPPLER (1894–1966)

Georg Keppler commanded a company during World War I. In postwar Germany, he joined the police and rose through the ranks as an officer and a criminal inspector, culminating in becoming chief of the *Schutzpolizei* in 1930. He joined the SS-VT in 1935 and was given command of the first battalion of *SS Standarte I Deutschland* on 10 October 1935. In early 1938, Keppler formed a primarily Austrian regiment, *Der Führer*. He commanded this unit with distinction during the battle with France, where he won the Knight's Cross.

In July 1941, Keppler took over command of *Totenkopf* from Matthias Kleinheisterkamp and led the division through some of its toughest fighting around Lake Ilmen, including the assault on the Luga Line. The division endured a terrible battle of attrition under his leadership. Eicke returned to take command in September of that year. Keppler, who had fallen ill through a brain tumour, spent the rest of the year recuperating. He was then appointed commander of *Das Reich*. He held this post until February 1943, when he was again forced from his command by illness. On his recovery, Keppler led 1st SS Panzer Corps through much of the Normandy campaign. He returned to the Eastern Front to lead 3rd SS Panzer Corps until February 1945. Despite his illness, Keppler was one of the SS's most able commanders.

HEINZ LAMMERDING (1905–1971)

Heinz Lammerding held two engineering degrees, which gained him employment in the Head Office of the Army's Training Department. After joining the Nazi party, however, he headed the SA Engineering School. On 1 April 1935, he joined the pioneer branch of the *SS-Verfügungstruppen* with the rank of *Obersturmführer* (lieutenant). He was later promoted to *Hauptsturmführer* (captain) and taught at the SS Officer's School at Braunschweig. He was then transferred to Eicke's concentration camp inspectorate.

In October 1939, Lammerding took over command of *Totenkopf*'s pioneer battalion, which he led with distinction in the French campaign of 1940. Lammerding was awarded the Knight's Cross – both

First Class and Second Class – for his bravery in this campaign, particularly for his role in repelling a British armoured counterattack near Arras. He performed similarly well during the invasion of the Soviet Union as Eicke's divisional operations officer. Lammerding played a key role in the battles to break the Stalin Line in the autumn of 1941 and also during the battles of the Demyansk encirclement. Very much Eicke's protégé, he was promoted to *Obersturmbannsturmführer* (lieutenant colonel) and given command of the division's motorcycle battalion. He led this unit through the successful battles around Kharkov in the winter of 1942–43, where he won the German Cross in Gold (an award bridging the gap between the Iron Cross First Class and the Knight's Cross). He also commanded the division for a short period between 27 April and 15 May 1943.

After a brief spell on the staff of 2nd SS Panzer Corps, Himmler personally selected Lammerding for the post of Chief of Staff for Erich von dem Bach-Zelewski's anti-partisan forces. Lammerding organised the clearing of Pripet marshes, which claimed the lives of at least 15,000 Soviet people. As a reward he was awarded the Knight's Cross and given command of the 2nd SS Panzer Division *Das Reich*. Max Hastings, author of the excellent history of that division in France in 1944, *Das Reich*, indicates that this was not due to Lammerding's skill as a commander, but rather to his close relationship with Himmler. However, his previous performance seems to have been competent and he was highly rated by Eicke, who was a difficult man to impress. Whatever the case, Lammerding brought the ruthless zeal he had shown in the Pripet marshes to the command of his new division, which was based in France.

In May 1944, he launched the infamous 'Blood and Ashes' offensive against the French Resistance in the Auverge and had 99 French suspects publicly hanged. In June of the same year, while the unit was en route to the Normandy beachhead, he sanctioned the killing of more than 600 French civilians, including 207 children, at Oradour-sur-Glane in reprisal for the killing of an SS officer. The division reached Normandy on 10 July 1944, where it faced the

Americans, who were attempting to drive inland. Lammerding was wounded on 26 July, but had recovered enough to return to the command *Das Reich* in November. He led the division during the ill-fated Ardennes Offensive and subsequently briefly held the command of the 38th SS Division *Nibelungen*. His final wartime post was as adjutant to Himmler. Although Lammerding was tried, convicted and sentenced to death in absentia by a French court after the war, he was never imprisoned. The French Government was still trying to extradite him from West Germany when he died in 1971.

MAX SIMON (1899–1961)

A protégé of Theodor Eicke and *Totenkopf* stalwart, Max Simon was a central figure in the *Totenkopf* division and became one of the SS's best field commanders. He was a corporal in the First Life Cuirassier Regiment during World War I, where he won both the Iron Cross First and Second Class. Like

Left: An *Untersturmführer* of the *Theodor Eicke* Regiment presents a suitably-decorated drum built by the Hitler Youth to the *Totenkopf*'s commander, *SS-Brigadeführer* Hellmuth Becker (left) in early 1945.

many others, Simon found readjusting to civilian life difficult after the war and served for a while with the *Freikorps*. In 1920, he joined the *Reichswehr* as a sergeant with the 16th Cavalry Regiment, where he served until his retirement in 1929.

After drifting through a number of jobs, he joined the *Allgemeine-SS* in 1933. He entered the camp inspectorate and, under Eicke's tutelage, progressed quickly to commander of the SS guard unit at Sachsenburg. In 1935, Eicke moved Simon to the *Oberbayen* regiment. On his promotion to *SS-Sturmbannführer* (major) in 1937, Eicke gave him command of the 1st Battalion of *SS-Totenkopfstandarte I Oberbayen*. Two months later, Simon took command of the regiment itself and took it to war in the Polish campaign. This formation later became part of the *Totenkopf* division in October 1939. He led the regiment in France and subsequently on the Eastern Front. His ability and ruthlessness earned him much praise and a Knight's Cross in October 1941. Simon also commanded the division at times of Eicke's absence and led elements of it that were cut off in the Demyansk pocket in February and March 1942. He took over the division in July 1943 following Heinz Lammerding's brief tenure after Eicke's death. Although he never commanded the same devotion that Eicke had enjoyed, he led the division in a similarly aggressive manner and achieved similar results.

On 16 October 1943, Simon took command of 16th SS Panzer Grenadier Division *Reichsführer-SS*. He led the division for just over a year and won the Oak Leaves to his Knight's Cross during this period. He ended the war heading 13th SS Army Corps in southwestern Germany. While the division was serving in Italy, he authorised the reprisal killings of 2700 Italian civilians on the Arno in August 1944. Simon was condemned to death for this crime by the British. There was another unsubstantiated Soviet sentence against him for the massacre of civilians around Kharkov,

although he is on record as saying that the Russians were 'bandits who must be slaughtered without pity'. The British death sentence was commuted and he was released in 1954. He was tried a further two times in Germany, but was acquitted. Simon died in 1961.

HERMANN PRIESS (1901–1985)

Hermann Priess was too young to serve in World War I, but joined the 18th Volunteer Dragoon Regiment in January 1919 and saw fighting on Germany's eastern border. He subsequently served in the *Reichswehr*. Priess joined the *SS-Verfügungstruppe* in 1934 and served with the *SS-Standarte Germania*. He joined *Totenkopf* and commanded an infantry regiment during Operation Barbarossa. Priess, however, was trained as an artilleryman and he took over *Totenkopf*'s Artillery Regiment 3 where he won the Knight's Cross. He briefly commanded the division after Eicke's death, but took over for a longer period from 22 October 1943 to 21 June 1944. The division's excellent performance during the winter of 1943–44 was a tribute to Priess's command abilities and he was rewarded with the Oak Leaves to his Knight's Cross in September 1943 and the Swords were awarded in April of the following year.

From July 1944, Priess led 1st SS Panzer Division *Leibstandarte Adolf Hitler* and was still in command of the division during the Ardennes Offensive. He later headed the 1st SS Panzer Corps during the last months of the war, seeing service in Hungary and Austria. He was arrested after the war and stood trial at Dachau for the massacre of captured American troops at Malmédy by troops from his division. He was sentenced to 20 years in prison, but was released in 1954. Priess died in 1985.

HELLMUTH BECKER (1902–1952)

Hellmuth Becker was *Totenkopf*'s last commander. Becker had served in the *Reichswehr* before joining *SS-Totenkopfstandarte I Oberbayen*. He commanded *Oberbayen*'s 1st battalion with considerable success in Poland and France, and was awarded the Iron Cross – both First Class and Second Class – despite being wounded. Eicke personally gave Becker command of

Left: **Sepp Dietrich was originally the commander of the** *Leibstandarte* **Adolf Hitler Division, but by the end of the war had risen to command the 6th SS Panzer Army, which took the lead role in Operation Spring Awakening.**

Right: **Heinrich Schuldt, Knight's Cross holder, was commander of SS Infantry Regiment 4** *Ostmark* **(formed from** *SS-Totenkopfstandarte* **4) when it was decimated on the Eastern Front in the winter of 1941. He was killed in 1944.**

one of *Totenkopf*'s infantry regiments for the Russian campaign, where he once again achieved considerable success in the Demyansk encirclement. He received the Knight's Cross in September 1943 and gained his Oak Leaves a year later.

Becker was very much Eicke's protégé and personal friend. Becker had the qualities that Eicke admired in a soldier: he was outstandingly brave and utterly ruthless. Becker did, however, possess a number of shortcomings, both sexual and military. Himmler, at the behest of a number of junior *Totenkopf* officers, launched an inquiry into Becker's misconduct prior to his appointment to command the division in July 1944. The investigation rumbled on throughout the war, but did not stop Becker from assuming his command. Hitler's personal admiration did much to ensure Becker suffered no punishment from the *Reichsführer*.

BECKER'S MISDEEDS

The allegations against him, however, were serious, particularly in the eyes of the prim Heinrich Himmler. They included charges of the public rape of Russian women and being insensibly drunk in front line command. His alleged actions when *Totenkopf* refitted in France in late 1942 were similarly outrageous. In the Christmas of 1942, he was purported to have organised and led an orgy in the regimental officers' canteen where he broke up furniture and then rode a horse to death in front of his fellow revellers. The regimental surgeon Dr Bockhorn claimed that Becker kept prostitutes in his forward command post in the Ukraine in 1943. He also said that, in April 1943, to celebrate Hitler's

birthday, Becker, while drunk, had ordered a 10-minute salvo by all the regiment's heavy guns in Hitler's honour, wasting scarce ammunition and forcing the men in adjacent units to seek cover.

Despite such behaviour, Becker held the division together through the increasingly difficult final months of the war and led it in attempt to relieve Budapest. He surrendered the *Totenkopf* Division to the American 3rd Army on 9 May 1945, but he and his division were handed over to the Red Army. Becker was sentenced to 25 years hard labour, but was executed by the Soviets in 1952 for allowing an unexploded grenade to be concreted into a wall.

CHAPTER EIGHT

FIREPOWER

Once the division had proven itself as a fighting unit in France, like the other *Waffen-SS* divisions, it was kept relatively well-supplied throughout the war, and could count on being one of the first units to receive the latest German combat equipment.

Traditionally, the division is the smallest formation in which all arms are combined. Although this was once cavalry, infantry and artillery, by World War II, in the case of the German panzer or panzer grenadier division, this meant it contained infantry, armour, anti-aircraft guns and artillery. These 'teeth' arms of the division were combined with supporting services, and were under the command of one man, making them capable of fighting independently.

It should be noted that some elements of the division were, to some extent, self-contained. Usually, in the case of the Germans, this would consist of a rifle regiment and a tank regiment with supporting engineers, signallers and an artillery battalion. Such formations were known as *Kampfgruppen*, or battle groups. Even before *Totenkopf* was converted from a motorised division to a panzer grenadier division, thereby receiving its first tanks, Eicke had already adopted the idea to increase the division's flexibility and firepower. During the interval between the end of the French campaign and the opening of Barbarossa, he reorganised the division into two

powerful battle groups. These were based around an infantry regiment and included attached companies or even whole battalions of engineers, communication personnel, anti-tank men, motorcyclists and fully motorised heavy and light artillery and anti-aircraft batteries. Eicke intended to deploy the two battle groups in front – although still behind the reconnaissance screen which always remained under divisional headquarters control, with the third infantry regiment and the remainder of the combat units some way back. These would be closely followed by the administrative and supply units.

The division and even the battle groups would operate a considerable range of weaponry, from small arms through to heavy artillery. *Totenkopf* was no exception and, once it converted to a panzer grenadier and subsequently panzer division, it also included tanks. This section aims to examine the key weapon systems operated by the division throughout the war. It is by no means comprehensive, given the bewildering variety of weapons typically used by *Waffen-SS* formations, and especially *Totenkopf*.

It should also be remembered that, despite the reputation of the SS as being a superbly equipped elite, initial formations such as *Leibstandarte*, the SS-VT and *Totenkopf* went to war extremely parlously equipped, due the army's resistance to the growth of

Left: The PzKpfw VI Tiger Ausf E armed with an 88mm L/56 Kwk 36 gun. These potent beasts served with *Totenkopf*'s heavy tank company at Kursk, where they successfully spearheaded the division's advance.

Left: A *Totenkopf SS-Sturmann* checks his Luger P08 9mm automatic pistol. This was a popular weapon on both sides, but had a very complex mechanism. Its 9mm ammunition was also used by German machine pistols.

the *Waffen-SS*. It was only once the original *Waffen-SS* divisions had proved themselves in the terrible fighting in the winter of 1941–42 in the Soviet Union that they began to receive the newest and best equipment. Even then, it was only the best divisions such as *Leibstandarte, Das Reich, Totenkopf, Wiking* and *Hitlerjugend* that were first in the queue. Thus the following selection is a confusing mixture of the obsolete and obsolescent, scavenged and scrounged foreign material, and the finest and most complex weaponry Nazi Germany could produce.

As Theodor Eicke strove to turn the *Totenkopfverbände* into viable combat units, the one class of weaponry he did not have particular problems obtaining was small arms. After all, it was perfectly logical that concentration guards should be reasonably well equipped with regard to rifles, pistols and machine guns. Those guns came from a variety of sources, however, and not all the weapons that *Totenkopf* went to war with in France in 1940 were of the most modern design.

PISTOLS

Handguns are of very limited use in modern warfare. They are comparatively inaccurate; even in the hands of marksmen, pistols are rarely effective at ranges of more than 40–50m (130–165ft) and, except at close range, are rarely lethal because of their small calibre. Furthermore, for such a small weapon, the pistol takes considerable industrial potential and skill to manufacture. Traditionally, it had also been a weapon of officers and senior NCOs. This meant that the carrier of a handgun was easily identified as such and a prime target for snipers. However, the propensity for SS officers to wear jodhpurs probably contributed more to this problem than carrying a pistol. Indeed, when *Totenkopfverbände* operated behind the German lines in Poland, a number of officers were shot by Polish snipers, who easily singled out the *Totenkopf*

officers in their distinctive dress and 'jaunty' insignia. During World War I, officers soon took to carrying rifles, which, quite apart from being more effective weapons, rendered the officers almost indistinguishable from their men. Junior *Totenkopf* officers adopted this practice and usually carried a machine pistol, as well as the traditional sidearm.

Nonetheless, handguns were issued in large numbers to the *Totenkopf* division. This was because, despite the reasons listed above, the pistol continued to play an important role. For many troops, carrying a larger personal weapon such as a rifle was out of the question. In the cramped confines of a vehicle, there was little space to stow anything other than a pistol. Yet, should the crew be forced to leave the vehicle in combat, they required some sort of weapon for self-defence. Furthermore, given the fact that the division was constantly operating in hostile territory, having even a small weapon always to hand was usually a sensible precaution. It should also be remembered that, in close-quarter combat such as trench clearance and urban warfare, possession of such a handy and easily aimed weapon was a positive benefit. Finally, despite everything, the pistol remained a status symbol and thus most staff officers, even if they were far from the battlefield, continued to strap pistols to themselves.

The German Army had adopted the semi-automatic pistol in favour of the revolver early in the twentieth century and, therefore, unlike many other contemporary armies, the revolver had an almost minimal presence in the *Wehrmacht*. The famous *Pistole* P'08, more widely known outside Germany as the Luger, was adopted as the German service pistol in 1908 and was used throughout World War I. It was extremely popular with the troops, as it was easy to handle and point, and usually extremely well made. Nonetheless, it was not ideally suited to trench warfare. Its complicated upward-opening toggle lock mechanism was prone to clog with dirt and mud. The Luger thus required considerable care and maintenance. It was also complicated and slow to manufacture. The Walther P38 therefore replaced it as the German service pistol in 1938. However, the Luger continued in parallel production until 1942 and gave sterling

service throughout World War II. (Note: All weights given empty.)

PISTOLE P '08
Cartridge: 9mm Parabellum
Length: 222mm
Weight: 0.877kg
Magazine capacity: 8-round box
Muzzle velocity: 320m/sec

Popular as the Luger was, it was not compatible with the increased military production required by the German war machine. Walther Waffenfabrik produced the excellent P38 in response to the need for a

Above: *Totenkopfverbände* **camp guards outside the main gates of Oranienburg concentration camp in 1933, shortly after Hitler had come to power. They are armed with the World War I vintage** *Gewehr* **98 rifle.**

more simply manufactured weapon. The P38 incorporated some excellent safety features, such as a double-action trigger which allowed the pistol to be carried securely with the safety catch off. Most importantly, it was robust and well liked by the troops. This was because the pistol sat well in the hand and had a crisp, clean trigger action, all of which enhanced its accuracy. The Walther action also kept out the dirt and dust. Perhaps most importantly, it continued to function in the extremes of climate on the Eastern Front. Indeed, when temperatures dropped to such low levels that gun oil froze, the gun could be kept free of oil and continue to function. The Walther P38 was so good that *SS-Oberführer* Gärtner, *chef des Beschaffungsamtes* (Chief of the SS Procurement Office) tried to divert the entire P38 production to the *Waffen-SS*, but was defeated in a long and bitter battle by the Army Weapons Department.

WALTHER P38
Cartridge: 9mm Parabellum
Length: 219mm
Weight: 0.960kg
Magazine capacity: 8-round box
Muzzle velocity: 350m/sec

Officers, particularly those unlikely to be involved directly in combat, usually preferred to carry something more compact. One should remember though that Eicke expected all officers in his division, however senior, to lead from the front. All major *Totenkopf* commanders and senior officers seem to have been personally very courageous, perhaps because the only crime on the battlefield Eicke seemed to have recognised was cowardice. Personal bravery was an essential prerequisite for those who wanted to advance in *Totenkopf*. This was personified by Eicke himself, who recklessly led the crossing of Le Bassée Canal on 24 May 1940 – pistol in hand – against concentrated British rifle and machine-gun fire. Nonetheless, most officers preferred to carry the smaller Walther PP or PPK pistols, which were also favoured by tank crews. Both were excellent and advanced designs worked on the blowback principle, and incorporated external hammers and double-action triggers and more than adequate safety features. They were easy to strip and maintain, and came in 9mm, 7.65mm and 6.35mm calibres. The main drawback was their somewhat limited range of 25–30m (80–100ft).

WALTHER PP
Cartridge: 9mm *kurz*/7.65mm/6.35mm
Length: 174mm

Weight: 0.682kg
Magazine: 8-round box
Muzzle velocity: 290m/sec

WALTHER PPK
Cartridge: 9mm kurz/7.65mm/6.35mm
Length: 155mm
Weight: 0.568kg
Magazine: 7-round box
Muzzle velocity: 280m/sec

As it expanded to division size in October 1939, *Totenkopf* received large numbers of Czech weapons from the arsenals taken over by the Germans in March 1939. Amongst these guns were a large number of Czech service pistols. However, unlike most Czech equipment, the 9mm *Automaticky Pistole* vz.38, produced by Ceska Zbrojovka in Prague, was not so well regarded. Known as the *Pistole* P38(t) in German service, it had a heavy double-action trigger pull and so was generally inaccurate.

PISTOLE P38(t)
Cartridge: 9mm kurz
Length: 198mm
Weight: 0.909kg
Magazine: 8-round box
Muzzle velocity: 296m/sec

SUBMACHINE GUNS
Easier to handle than a rifle, capable of producing large volumes of automatic fire and relatively compact, the submachine gun, termed the machine pistol by the Germans, reigned supreme in close-quarter fighting. Within *Totenkopf* formations, junior officers, NCOs, special assault squads, combat engineers and specialists were equipped with machine pistols. Also, most larger combat vehicles had enough space for the stowage of at least one such weapon. Initially at least, *Totenkopf* did not have access to the latest designs, which went straight to the army. Machine pistol-armed *Totenkopf* personnel went into battle in France carrying versions of the Bergmann family of machine pistols. The Bergmann MP28 was a direct

descendant of the World War I Bergmann MP18, differing only in the provision of a single-shot capability, a few internal changes and a box magazine, which protruded from the left. *Totenkopf* also used the next generation of Bergmann machine pistol, the MP35. The MP35 had a new double-pressure system of rate of fire control; light pressure produced single shots and full pressure automatic.

Manufactured to an extremely high standard with walnut furniture, these were excellent, reliable weapons. The MP35 was a product of a different age, however, and too difficult to mass-produce in the numbers required for the army. Despite this, it remained in manufacture until 1945, all of which went to the *Waffen-SS*.

MP28

Calibre: 9mm Parabellum
Length: 815mm
Weight: 5.245kg
Magazine capacity: 32-round box
Cyclic rate of fire: 350–450rpm
Muzzle velocity: 365m/sec

MP35

Calibre: 9mm Parabellum
Length: 840mm
Weight: 4.73kg
Magazine capacity: 24- or 32-round box
Cyclic rate of fire: 650rpm
Muzzle velocity: 365m/sec

After the French campaign, *Totenkopf* began to receive newer weapons and the MP38, the most famous German submachine gun of the war, was something very different to the Bergmann guns. While not particularly innovative as a gun, it was revolutionary in terms of the mass production methods used in its manufacture. The MP38 was constructed from metal stampings, die-cast parts and plastic furniture; it was simple, but also robust and effective. Its manufacture was further simplified in 1940 and the resulting weapon was known as the MP40. To the troops who rightly prized this reliable and handy weapon, this

change would have made little noticeable difference. Incidentally, the MP-38/MP-40's nickname, the 'Schmeisser', is something of a misnomer, as Hugo Schmeisser had nothing to do with the Erma-designed weapon.

MP40

Calibre: 9mm Parabellum
Length: 83.3cm
Weight: 4.1kg
Magazine capacity: 32-round box
Cyclic rate of fire: 500rpm
Muzzle velocity: 365m/sec

Totenkopf troops also were not averse to using Soviet PPSh 41s. These robust weapons were captured in such vast numbers that they eventually became the second-most common machine pistol in German service and many were even chambered to their own 9mm ammunition.

RIFLES

The standard weapon of all *Totenkopf* men and all *Waffen-SS* and army troops would have been the Mauser-designed *Karabiner* 98k, although the older, less handy World War I veteran, the *Gewehr* 98, often saw service, too, particularly with pre-war *Totenkopfverbände* troops. The 7.92mm bolt-action 98k was a sturdy, reliable service rifle and accurate up to 925m (1000yds).

KARABINER 98K

Calibre: 7.92mm
Length: 1107.5cm
Weight: 3.9kg
Magazine capacity: 5-round box
Muzzle velocity: 755m/sec

All the armies of the major participants of World War II, with the exception of the United States, went to war with bolt-action rifles as the main personal weapon of their infantry. Yet, by 1940, the Wehrmacht had identified the need for a self-loading rifle to increase the firepower of the troops. The

German attempts to produce such a rifle, the *Gewehr* 41(w) and *Gewehr* 43, did not make a particularly large impact on weapon design. The Soviet SVT40 – which was its inspiration – and the American Garand M1 were easily better rifles. The StG44, however, was one of the most influential firearms of World War II, as it was the first modern assault rifle. German after-action studies came to the conclusion that most infantry combat took place under ranges of 400m (430yds), yet the German soldier was carrying a rifle that was accurate above 1000m (1093yds). The infantry would be better armed with something that combined the firepower and handiness of a submachine gun in the assault and could fire accurate selective fire in defence. Early experiments using the 7.92mm rifle cartridge proved a failure, as such powerful ammunition was too much of a handful when fired on automatic.

Above: SS-Standartenführer **Felix Steiner, commander of** *SS-VT Standarte Deutschland* **in Poland, 1939. The man in the foreground is armed with the Bergmann MP28, the standard machine pistol in** *Waffen-SS* **service at that time.**

The Haenel team under Louis Schmeisser, however, developed the *Maschinenkarbiner* 42(H), which fired a new *kurz* (short) 7.92mm cartridge that, although it resembled the equivalent rifle round, was shortened and contained less propellant. It lacked the range of the traditional cartridge, but at most combat ranges up to 600m (650yds) was more than adequate; most importantly, it could be comfortably handled during full automatic fire. Trials were undertaken on the Eastern Front, where it was initially known as the *Maschinenpistole* 43 or MP43 to disguise it from Hitler's notice, as he disapproved of the assault rifle programme. Small numbers were issued to the

Waffen-SS Divisions *Leibstandarte, Das Reich* and *Totenkopf* in late 1942. The troops involved in the trial waxed lyrical about the new weapon and its reputation was sealed when, according to legend, a batch of the new rifles was dropped to a German unit surrounded by Soviet formations. Using the MP43, they proceeded to fight their way out of the encirclement. Eventually such was demand from the army for the new gun that Hitler relented from his earlier opposition and bestowed on it a more suitable name, the *Sturmgewehr* (assault rifle) 44 or StG44.

The StG44 represented a quantum leap in an infantryman's firepower compared to his bolt-action rifle armed counterpart. It revolutionised tactics, making a squad far less dependent on supporting fire from machine guns as they carried their own fire support with them. The rifle was highly sought after and, despite its ease of manufacture, only went to elite units such as the SS. Even with such formations as *Totenkopf*, its issue was limited to the very best assault platoons and companies.

StG44
Calibre: 7.92mm (kurz)
Length: 940mm
Weight: 5.22kg
Cyclic rate of fire: 500rpm
Magazine: 30-round box
Muzzle velocity: 650 m/sec

MACHINE GUNS

Central to all German infantry tactics was the squad's machine gun. As long as SS men could keep the majority of their machine guns intact, they could hold off vastly superior infantry forces. These tactics were made possible by the excellence of the two major German machine-gun designs of World War II. Although many armies retained their World War I heavy machine guns (the ageing German MG-08 saw extensive service, including its use by *Totenkopf*'s *Heimwehr Danzig* Regiment in Poland in 1939), most had a separate, light machine-gun design such as the British Bren or American BAR as the squad support weapon. In the mid-1930s, the Germans developed

Right: Knight's Cross winner Erwin Meierdrees (right) standing beside a knocked-out T-34 on the Eastern Front. His companion is carrying an MP40 submachine gun in his left hand.

the new concept of the general-purpose machine gun. They produced a gun that was light enough to be carried by one man and used in the assault role, but, when mounted on a tripod, could produce the volume of fire of a heavy machine gun. This was the Rheinmetall *Maschinengewehr* 34 or MG34, the finest weapon of its generation. For squad work, it was mounted on a biped and fed by either belts or a 75-round saddle drum. Fitted to a Lafette-34 tripod, it was capable of accurate and sustained fire at ranges of more than 3000m (3240yds). The MG34 was also commonly used on vehicle mounts such as the standard armament of infantry carrying SdKfz 251 half-tracks and as an anti-aircraft weapon. It really was an excellent machine gun, capable of astounding rates of fire, but, to quote one small arms expert: 'The design was really too good for military use. It took too long to manufacture and involved too many complex and expensive machining processes. The result was a superb weapon, but actually using it was rather like using a Rolls Royce car for ploughing a field – it was too good for the task.'

MG34
Calibre: 7.92mm
Length: 1219mm
Weight: 11.5kg (with bipod)
Cyclic rate of fire: 800–900rpm
Feed: 50-round belts (usually linked together in 5 x 50-round belt lengths) or 75-round drum

The Mauser design team produced a cheaper and simpler weapon than the MG34, which was even more suited to its purpose. The *Maschinengewehr* 42 or MG42, nicknamed the 'Spandau' by Allied troops, was probably the finest machine gun of World War II. While it was rugged and well able to stand up to the rigours of service life, what was most extraordinary about the MG42 was its phenomenal

Left: A *Totenkopf* MG34 machine gun team in the early stages of Operation Barbarossa, the invasion of the Soviet Union. The MG34 was a superlative machine gun, but was complex and expensive to manufacture.

rate of fire – up to 1500 rounds a minute. It could go through a 250-round belt in less than 15 seconds. This was double to three times the rate of most Allied weapons and the noise of a MG42 firing has been compared to that of a band saw or tearing linoleum. Such a rate of fire meant that the machine gun's barrel had to be regularly changed and this could be done in less than five seconds. It was distributed widely from the end of 1942 onwards and meant that *Waffen-SS* formations such as *Totenkopf* could put up prodigious amounts of fire in defence.

MG42
Calibre: 7.92mm
Length: 1220mm
Weight: 11.5kg
Cyclic rate of fire: up to 1550rpm
Feed: 50-round belt

It should be noted, however, that, once again, when *Totenkopf* was blooded in France, the vast majority of machine guns came from Czech sources. Fortunately, these weapons were very good indeed. They were two light machine guns, the ZB vz 26 and ZB vz.30 (known in German service as the MG26(t) and MG30(t), respectively). Both fired the standard German 7.92mm cartridge and used 30-round box magazines. These guns were the basis of the famous British Bren Gun. If they had any flaws, it was their difficulty of manufacture. *Totenkopf* also used older and heavier Czech machine guns.

MG30(t)
Calibre: 7.92mm
Length: 1161mm
Weight: 10.04kg
Cyclic rate of fire: 500rpm
Feed: 30-round box

ANTI-TANK RIFLES

At the start of the war, the principal infantry anti-armour weapon in Western armies was the anti-tank rifle. The standard German anti-tank rifle was the 7.92 *Panzerbüchse* 39. It equipped *Totenkopf* infantry and anti-tank units in the French campaign. Originally, it fired 7.92mm ammunition with a hard steel core, but examination of captured Polish weapons led to the Germans introducing a tungsten core, which improved penetration. Nonetheless, the anti-tank rifle was still rendered increasingly obsolete by heavier tank armour. The single-shot rifle could penetrate 25mm (1in) of armour at 300m (320yds) and thus was unable to tackle any but the lightest tanks after 1940, and the lack of any weapon able of dealing with the heavier British and French tanks seriously affected *Totenkopf* morale.

PzB 39
Calibre: 7.92mm
Length: 1620mm overall
Weight: 12.6kg
Armour penetration: 25mm at 300m

ANTI-TANK GUNS

As Eicke set about expanding *Totenkopf* into a division, he finally received his first anti-tank guns for his tank hunter (*panzerjäger*) battalion from the army depot at Kassel in mid-November 1939. These were 16 37mm Pak 35/36 guns. Although the gun had proved successful during the Polish campaign, when it faced more heavily armoured British and French tanks in 1940, the crews often watched in horror as their armoured piercing shells bounced off the enemy tanks. When *Totenkopf* anti-tank gunners faced British Matilda tanks at Arras on 20 May 1940, the tanks proved impervious to the Pak 35/36, even at point-blank range, and the inexperienced gunners broke and fled. The Pak 35/36 also saw use in the 1941 campaign in the Soviet Union because no larger calibre replacement had been produced in time. The Pak 36 proved utterly hopeless against the T-34 and earned the derisive nickname the 'doorknocker'. This was amply illustrated when the Soviets launched a heavy armoured counterattack against *Totenkopf* at Lushno on the Pola River. Again, the gun proved useless against T-34s and KV-Is and the situation was only saved by the divisional artillery firing at the Soviet tanks over open sights.

PAK 36

Calibre: 37mm
Length: 1665mm
Weight: 328kg
Maximum range: 7000m
Armour penetration: 38mm at 30 degrees at 365m

The replacement for the Pak 36 was the 5cm Pak 38, which began to be supplied to the troops in 1941, much to relief of formations such as *Totenkopf.* It proved, when equipped with tungsten-core ammunition, to be the only gun capable of penetrating the T-34's armour; without it, the T-34 had to be within 500m (540yds). The division had a few Pak 38s at Lushno and they proved utterly vital. Indeed, *SS-Sturmmann* (Corporal) Fritz Christen won a Knight's Cross for his heroic use of the 5cm Pak 38 in the face of overwhelming numbers of Soviet tanks. He was the first and youngest enlistee to win this award.

PAK 38

Calibre: 50mm
Length: 3187mm
Weight: 1000kg
Maximum range: 2650m
Armour penetration (tungsten ammunition):
    101mm at 740m

The increasing thickness of Soviet tank armour meant that something heavier was needed than the 5cm Pak 38 gun, although it was an adequate anti-tank weapon. Consequently, Rheinmetall-Borsig came up with a new design that was essentially an

Right: A 37mm Pak 35/36 pulled by a *Kettenkrad* half-track motorcycle. Despite its success in Poland, the Pak 35/36 proved utterly inadequate against both the French and British and later Soviet tanks it faced.

up-scaled version of the 50mm gun in a larger 75mm calibre. The result was the 75mm Pak 40, which, naturally enough, resembled a larger version of its smaller sibling. It was also an excellent gun, capable of dealing with virtually any tank used by the Allies on all fronts throughout the war. German anti-tank gun-

ners rated it their best weapon and it was flexible enough in its range ammunition to make a reasonable artillery piece when firing high-explosive shells. First and foremost, however, it was a formidable anti-tank weapon. Using (all too rare) tungsten-core AP-40 ammunition, it could penetrate 98mm of amour

plating at 2000m (2180yds). At the more typical combat range of 500m (540yds), this increased to 154mm. In August 1942, *Totenkopf*'s tank destroyer battalion received its first batch of these potent guns when it rebuilt as a panzer grenadier division in the wake of the unit's virtual destruction in the Demyansk pocket.

PAK 40

Calibre: 75mm

Length: 3700mm

Weight: 1425kg

Maximum range: (High Explosive) 7680m

Armour penetration (tungsten ammunition): 98mm at 2000m

PORTABLE ANTI-TANK WEAPONS

As anti-tank rifles and the 37mm Pak 35/36 proved incapable of dealing with the best Soviet tanks, *Totenkopf* was forced to improvise in order to stop the Soviet armour. Eicke created special tank annihilation squads, who hunted tanks on foot armed with a mix of satchel charges, mines, petrol bombs and grenades. *SS-Hauptsturmführer* (Captain) Max Seela and his squad achieved a formidable reputation as expert tank-killers using these methods in the fighting at Lushno.

The first really effective hand-held anti-tank weapon was the *Panzerfaust*, which appeared in late 1942. It was a simple tubular projector, which fired a hollow charge grenade and was discarded after use. The first introduced was the *Panzerfaust* 30 (the number 30 referred to the 30m range of the weapon). The short range was a considerable tactical disadvantage to the firer, who required steady nerves to achieve a hit – although a *Panzerfaust* hit usually proved lethal to any tank. Later models such as the *Panzerfaust* 60 and the *Panzerfaust* 100 increased the range. Virtually any Allied tank was vulnerable to this weapon and it was much feared by Allied tank crews. All SS panzer grenadiers were heavily issued with this weapon.

PANZERFAUST 30

Range: 30m

Weight: Total – 5.2kg; warhead – 3kg

Armour penetration: 200mm

PANZERFAUST 60

Range: 60m

Weight: Total – 6.8kg; warhead – 3kg

Armour penetration: 200mm

Right: The 75mm Pak 40 anti-tank gun. This was an excellent anti-tank gun able to deal with almost any Allied armour. It could also be used as a field artillery piece, firing high explosive shells.

PANZERSCHRECK

In 1943, the Germans captured a number of US M1 bazookas. The Germans quickly produced a much-improved rocket launcher, the 88mm *Raketenpanzerbüchse* 43. It was an immediate success as an anti-tank weapon and could penetrate 160mm of tank armour at about 150m (160yds). It gave off a considerable blast of gas and debris when fired and, on the original version, the operator had to wear protective clothing. An improved version, the RPzB 54, had a shield to protect the firer. It was operated by two men and panzer grenadiers often carried extra ammunition for the RPzB in special racks on the sides of their SdKfz 251 half-tracks. The weapon was often nicknamed the *Panzerschrek*.

RPzB 54

Calibre: 88mm

Weight: With shield – 11kg; rocket – 3.5kg

Length: 1638mm

Range: 150m

Rate of fire: 4–5rpm

MORTARS

The mortar is essentially a high-elevation, smooth-bore weapon which fires its fin-stabilised bomb in a high plunging trajectory. It is light and therefore mobile, and thus able to provide flexible indirect fire support in both defence and attack. *Totenkopf* infantry/grenadier companies would usually have two or three 50mm or 80mm mortars. The Germans made themselves masters in the handling of mortars and were experts at bringing down mortar barrages on Allied positions. In the first years of World War II, the standard platoon weapon was the 50mm *leichte Granatwerfer* 36 (leGrW 36), which *Totenkopf* used in France. It was a light, overly complex weapon and was phased out in favour of better models later in the war.

leGrW 36

Calibre: 50mm
Length: Barrel – 465mm; bore – 350mm
Weight: 14kg
Maximum range: 520m
Projectile weight: 0.9kg

The 80mm *schwere Granatwerfer* 34 (sGrW 34) held a fearsome reputation amongst Allied troops for its accuracy and its rate of fire. Despite its reputation, it was not a particularly remarkable weapon; rather, it was the training of the German mortar crews that made it so effective. It could fire high-explosive and smoke bombs, and could be mounted for use from SdKfz 250/7 half-tracks.

sGrW 34

Calibre: 81.4mm
Length: Barrel – 1143mm; bore – 1033mm
Weight: 56.7kg
Maximum range: 2400m
Projectile weight: 3.5kg

INFANTRY GUNS

German tactical doctrine required that each infantry battalion have artillery support available to it at all times. Special light guns were known to be particularly valuable in this role. The standard weapon in this category was the 75mm *leichte Infantriegeschütz* 18 (leIG 18), which entered service in 1932. A panzer grenadier battalion's heavy company in a division such as *Totenkopf* might have one- or two-gun 75mm leIG 18 support sections. The gun proved sturdy and reliable, even though it had a limited range because of its short barrel. The leIG 18 was supposed to have an anti-tank capability using hollow-charge ammunition, but this was ineffective and was little used.

75mm leIG 18

Calibre: 75mm
Length overall: 900mm
Weight: 400kg
Maximum range: 3550m
Projectile weight: 5.45 or 6kg (HE)

Waffen-SS support companies also used heavy weapons such as the 150mm *schwere Infantriegeschütz 33* (sIG 33). It was an orthodox if somewhat heavy weapon. Although it was ideally mounted on a self-propelled carriage and thus corresponded with the originator of blitzkrieg Heinz Guderian's ideas of mobile artillery instantly ready to support the tanks in action, in reality the sIG 33 was very often towed by truck or tractor. Typical self-propelled mounts were the SdKpf 138/1 or the PzKpfw I chassis (the only self-propelled artillery available to the German forces during the French campaign). In this role, it proved a useful support weapon and it stayed in service throughout the war.

150mm sIG 33
Calibre: 149.1mm
Length: Barrel – 1650mm
Weight: 1750kg
Maximum range: 4700m
Projectile weight: 38kg (HE)

FIELD ARTILLERY AND HOWITZERS

Perhaps, the most difficult task that Eicke faced in equipping *Totenkopf* between 1939 and 1940 was finding field artillery. In the face of army intransigence, he managed to get hold of enough Czech Skoda 100mm *houfnice* vz14/19 howitzers for *Totenkopf*'s light artillery battalions. Under the

German designation of 100mm leFH 14/19(t), these saw *Totenkopf* through the French campaign.

100mm leFh 14/19(t)
Calibre: 100mm
Length: 2400mm
Weight: 1505kg
Range: 9970m
Projectile weight: 14kg

The standard German field howitzer, however, was the 105mm *leichte Feldhaubitze* 16 (leFH 16), which was issued to *Totenkopf*'s artillery regiment's light battalions in preparation for the Russian campaign. It was a sound and sturdy piece with a useful range and weight of shell. It was perhaps rather too sturdy because its considerable weight meant that the 105mm leFH 16 could not be dragged out of the all-prevailing mud in Russia when the weather worsened.

105mm leFh 18/40
Calibre: 105mm
Length: 3310mm
Weight: 1955kg
Range: 12,325m
Projectile weight: 14.81kg

When it came to heavy artillery, Eicke had even more trouble. The army resolutely refused him the 150mm guns that he so desired for *Totenkopf*'s heavy artillery battalion. He even threatened to steal some 150mm guns that he had heard were lying unused at the Skoda works at Pilsen. The main problem was that the army refused to release the heavy artillery to the *Waffen-SS* until it had equipped the seventh and eighth wave of infantry divisions. The SS understandably took umbrage at this because these were third-rate *Landwehr* (reserve) divisions, whereas the *Waffen-SS* formations were going to be in the vanguard

Left: German troops train with the RPzB 54 88mm *Panzerschreck* in the summer of 1944. It was a formidable anti-tank weapon, but produced a large backblast when fired, which could reveal the operator's position.

of the attack on France. Eicke finally managed to get hold of his longed-for 150mm guns by direct intervention with Colonel General Weichs, who commanded the 2nd Army of which *Totenkopf* was a part. On 2 April 1940, Eicke staged a dazzling tour and display of his division to the general, who had not yet seen any SS formations. After the conclusion of a superlatively executed excise, Eicke asked the obviously impressed Weichs if he would be able to help in 'clearing up a few difficulties that had arisen about getting the necessary number of heavy guns' for *Totenkopf*'s heavy artillery section. Weichs agreed and soon made good his promise; four 150mm guns arrived in the middle of the month. They were ready for firing on 26 April, just two weeks before the French campaign opened. However, it was only in June 1941 that *Totenkopf* received its long-promised allotment of twelve 150mm artillery pieces, thus finally allowing Eicke to form a separate heavy battalion in his artillery regiment.

Germany's heavy field howitzer was the 150mm *schwere Feldhaubitze* 18 (sFH 18). It was a reliable and sound piece, although on the Eastern Front, the Germans found that it was outranged by the Soviet 152mm equivalent. As the war went on, the sFH 18 was placed on a self-propelled carriage known as the *Hummel*, and served as the mobile artillery in a number of panzer and panzer grenadier divisions.

150mm sFH 18
Calibre: 149mm
Length: 4440mm
Weight: 5512kg
Maximum range: 13,325m
Projectile weight: 43.5kg

Totenkopf received a battery of 105mm *schwere Kanone* 18 guns in 1942. The K–18 was a long-calibred gun intended for counter battery fire. These artillery pieces were far from satisfactory, being really far too heavy for the weight of shell fired. Admittedly, the 105mm K-18 had a very decent range, but it was only in service because other weapons were not available in the necessary numbers.

105mm K-18
Calibre: 105mm
Length: 5460mm
Weight: 5624kg
Range: 19,075m
Projectile weight: 15.14kg

ANTI-AIRCRAFT GUNS

As already noted, the *Totenkopf* Division was an all arms formation. Although its complement of anti-aircraft guns was small at the start of the war, experience soon taught the German armed forces as a whole to include more and more, and heavier and heavier, anti-aircraft guns in their divisions. By later in the war, considerable integral anti-aircraft firepower was wielded by *Totenkopf*. In the wake of the French campaign, it was already clear that a wide variety and large number of anti-aircraft guns were needed. In April 1941, Himmler authorised the formation of a full-sized flak battalion for *Totenkopf*. Eicke picked trained gunners from his artillery and infantry units, and sent them to Dachau, where the flak battalion was organised and trained. This battalion joined the division at the end of May, providing Eicke with fully motorised 12-piece batteries of 20mm and 30mm flak and a four-piece battery of the famous high-velocity 88mm flak gun. When *Totenkopf* was rebuilt as a panzer grenadier division after its terrible losses in the Demyansk encirclement, its anti-aircraft capacity was expanded still further. Hitler ordered that the division should receive a whole raft of new anti-aircraft guns organised into three batteries: one of 88mm, one of 50mm and one of 37mm guns, on top of a battery of 20mm pieces.

Although machine guns also provided local air defence, the lightest calibre dedicated air defence weapons were of 20mm calibre. The most common German design was the 20mm Flak 38, which could pump out the rounds at 420 to 480 per minute. It could also be used against ground targets. In 1940, to further increase the effectiveness of these weapons, the 20mm *Flakvierling* 38 was developed. This was simply a Flak 38 carriage modified to take four barrels. This combination proved dreadfully effective

against low-flying Allied aircraft. These quad 20mm guns were often mounted on vehicles such as SdKfz 7/1 half-tracks to provide more mobile air defence.

FLAK 38
Calibre: 20mm
Length: 2252.5mm
Weight: 420kg

Effective ceiling: 2200m
Rate of fire: 420–480rpm

The medium-calibre anti-aircraft gun used by the German Army was the 37mm Flak 36. A sound and effective weapon, the Flak 36 was fed by six round clips and could also be used against ground targets if necessary. It was difficult to produce, however, and

Above: Two *Waffen-SS* men with a selection of weaponry. The man in the foreground has a *Karabinier* 98k with a telescopic scope attached. A *Panzerfaust* rocket lies beside him. His companion is armed with a submachine gun.

Rheinmetall-Borsig introduced the 37mm Flak 43, which, by using stampings and prefabricated parts, could be produced in a quarter of the time of its predecessor. It also had the added advantage of a quicker rate of fire. In an effort to produce a more effective weapon, a twin barrel version, the 37mm *Flakzwilling* was produced. Both versions were extremely potent guns.

FLAK 36
Calibre: 37mm
Length: 3626mm
Weight: 1550kg
Effective ceiling: 4800m
Rate of fire: 160rpm

FLAK 43
Calibre: 37mm
Length: 3300mm
Weight: 1392kg
Effective ceiling: 4800m
Rate of fire: 420–480rpm

The lighter anti-aircraft guns of the division – the 20mm and 37mm – struggled to reach aircraft flying between 1500m (4850ft) and 3000m (9700ft). For the 88mm anti-aircraft guns, these heights were really too low. In an effort to plug the gap, Rheinmetall-Borsig designed the 50mm Flak 41, which entered German service in 1941. It was not the most successful of guns, however, as it was underpowered, too heavy and produced prodigious recoil and flash when fired. It was loaded with awkward five-clip magazine and overall the gun was never very popular.

FLAK 41
Calibre: 50mm
Length: 4686mm
Weight: 3kg
Effective ceiling: 3050m
Rate of fire: 180rpm

The heaviest anti-aircraft weapons in the division's arsenal were the guns of the 88mm Flak series, the Flak 18, Flak 36 and Flak 37. Quite apart from being excellent flak guns, they were often pressed into service as anti-tank guns, where their high muzzle veloc-ity and heavy projectile made an ideal tank-killer. However, the gun was really too high and bulky to be used comfortably in this role, although its range and power mitigated this somewhat.

FLAK 18
Calibre: 88mm
Weight: 5150kg
Length: 7.62m
Effective ceiling: 8000m

ARMOURED FIGHTING VEHICLES

At the outbreak of war, a motorised infantry division such as *Totenkopf* was exactly that – a division that been given trucks and motorcycles, and therefore no longer had to rely on the traditional method of foot and hoof for its mobility. In the summer of 1942, however, as it became evident that the division would have to be reconstructed after Demyansk and the subsequent period it remained in the line – like a number of the motorised infantry divisions – *Totenkopf* was allocated a battalion of tanks, which greatly increased the division's firepower. *Totenkopf* was to receive two companies of *Panzerkampfwagen* (PzKpfw) IIIs and a company of PzKpfw IVs. The army resisted handing over the tanks, claiming the demands of the Eastern Front and North Africa over-rode *Totenkopf*'s needs. This did not delay Eicke from forming a tank battalion for long, as Hitler overruled the army and ordered that *Totenkopf* should receive a company of the new heavy Tiger tanks. It was a vastly stronger and expanded *Totenkopf* that returned to the fray in March 1943. Conversion to a panzer grenadier division in 1943 also meant that *Totenkopf* gained SdKfz 251 half-tracked armoured personnel carriers to transport at least a proportion of its infantry/panz-er grenadiers. In October 1943, *Totenkopf* converted to an SS Panzer Division and, as one of the best SS divisions, continued to receive the latest tanks, assault guns and tank destroyers.

TANKS

The tank that *Totenkopf* received in the greatest numbers in the summer of 1942 was the PzKpfw III

Above: A 150mm sFH 18 howitzer of *Totenkopf*'s artillery regiment fires on Soviet positions. Eicke had to ask General Weichs to intervene on his behalf to obtain his first four heavy guns for the division.

Ausf L. It was descended from the early PzKpfw III, which entered service in September 1939. The medium tank had been up-armoured and up-gunned in each successive model over the two and half years of war. By the Model L, the PzKpfw had considerably thicker armour and a powerful, long 50mm KwK L/60 gun. It was largely with these that *Totenkopf* fought at Kharkov, although they were evidently outclassed by the Soviet T-34. In preparation for Kursk in the summer, the division also received new PzKpfw III Model Ms. The PzKpfw III did not see much more ser-

vice after Kursk and was steadily withdrawn from the autumn of 1943 onwards.

Pz Kpfw III Ausf M

Crew: 5
Weight: 22,300kg
Length: Incl. gun – 6.41m; hull – 5.52m
Width: 2.95m
Height: 2.50m
Armour: 50mm front plus 20mm
Armament: 50mm KwK 39 L/60 cannon, 2 x 7.92mm MG
Powerplant: Maybach HL 120 12-cylinder petrol engine – 140hp
Performance: Speed (road) – 40kmh; range (road) – 175km

The real workhorse of the German panzer forces was PzKpfw IV, which remained in production throughout the war and, continually up-gunned and up-armoured, gave excellent and reliable service. The PzKpfw IV was the commonest tank in German armoured formations. It was a match for most Allied tanks when armed with the long-barrelled 75mm KwK 40 L/48. Despite the increased strain put on the powerplant by increases in armour, it remained a vehicle with good mobility. Along with its PzKpfw IIIs, *Totenkopf* received new PzKpfw IV Ausf G and F2 tanks in the summer of 1942. These tanks proved clearly superior to the PzKpfw IIIs in the fighting around Kharkov. *Totenkopf* received a number of Model Hs in time for Kursk. The PzKpfw IV remained in service until the end of the war.

Pz Kpfw IV Ausf H
Crew: 5
Weight: 25,000kg
Length: Incl. gun – 7.02m; hull – 5.89m
Width: 3.29m

Above: A 37mm flak gun of a *Waffen-SS* **flak battery in the Soviet Union. Note the crew member with a range finder on the left of the photograph.** *Totenkopf's* **flak contingent became larger as the war progressed.**

Height: 2.68m
Armour: 70mm front, 30mm sides
Armament: 75mm KwK 40 L/48 gun, 2 x 7.92mm MG
Powerplant: Maybach HL 120 12-cylinder petrol engine – 300hp
Performance: Speed (road) – 24kmh; range (road) 200km

The PzKpfw V Panther was developed in response to the T-34 and KV-1. It was arguably the best tank of the conflict and combined fearsome firepower, excellent armour protection and reasonable mobility. The tank, however, was overly complex, which led to numerous mechanical failures and slowed production. Nonetheless, it was a superb tank in the increasingly defensive war *Totenkopf* had to fight.

Totenkopf received its first Panther Ausf Ds in late July and August 1943 after the debacle at Kursk. Hitler later decreed that the crack SS Panzer Divisions, including *Totenkopf*, should receive an entire battalion of Panthers. Thus the Panther in its later Ausf A and G models was the mainstay of *Totenkopf*'s tank force until the end of the war.

PzKpfw V Panther Ausf A

Crew: 5
Weight: 45,500kg
Length: Incl. gun – 8.86m; hull – 6.88m
Width: 23.43m
Height: 3.10m
Armour: 80mm front, 45mm sides

Below: Panzer grenadiers chat with a member of a Tiger's tank crew during the preparations for the Kursk offensive in mid-1943. After the battle, when it became a panzer division, *Totenkopf* was primarily equipped with Panthers.

Armament: 75mm KwK 42 L/70 cannon, 2 x 7.92mm MG
Powerplant: Maybach HL 230 P 30 12-cylinder engine – 700hp
Performance: Speed (road) – 46kmh; range (road) – 177km

As *Totenkopf* completed its conversion to a panzer grenadier division in 1943, it received a single heavy panzer company of 14 Tiger tanks. For its time, the Tiger was an outstanding tank design with good protection and an awesomely powerful 88mm gun. However, it was not able to turn the tide of the battle of Kursk. *Totenkopf*'s Tiger company fought hard through 1943 to early 1944, when *Totenkopf*'s heavy tanks were withdrawn.

Pz Kpfw VI Tiger Ausf E

Crew: 5
Weight: 55,000kg

Length: Incl. gun – 8.24m; hull – 6.2m
Width: 3.73m
Height: 2.86m
Armour: 100mm front, 60–80mm sides
Armament: 88mm KwK 36 L/56 gun, 2 x 7.92mm
  machine guns
Powerplant: Maybach HL 230 P45 12-cylinder
  petrol engine – 700hp
Performance: Speed (road) – 38kmh; range
  (road) – 100km

TANK DESTROYERS AND SELF PROPELLED GUNS

In an effort to provide German troops with armoured close-fire support, the *Sturmgeschütz* assault gun III was introduced into the German arsenal. With a low silhouette and reasonable armour, the 75mm cannon-armed StuG III soon proved itself very useful in battle. It began to be issued to *Waffen-SS* divisions *Leibstandarte*, *Das Reich* and *Totenkopf* in the spring of 1941, in preparation for Operation Barbarossa. Thus

the first armour these *Waffen-SS* divisions operated in World War II was not tanks, but turretless assault guns. Although the StuG III was intended as an infantry support weapon, it was inevitably used in an anti-tank role. Thus, later variants operated a longer calibre 75mm gun and were up-armoured, such as Model G; these played a key role for *Totenkopf* at Kharkov and Kursk.

StuG III
Crew: 4
Weight: 23,900kg
Length: 6.77m
Width: 2.95m
Height: 2.16m

Below: A StuG III with long-barrelled 75mm gun in the Soviet Union in September 1943. It was a useful addition to *Totenkopf*'s armoured strength, and the StuG III proved popular due to its low silhouette and thick armour.

Armament: 1 x 75mm gun, 2 x 7.92mm machine guns
Powerplant: 1 Maybach V12 – 265hp
Performance: Speed (road) – 40kmh; range (road) – 165km

The way in which the StuG III evolved from assault gun to tank destroyer set a pattern for a new breed of turretless armoured fighting vehicles which were also easier and quicker to produce than traditional tanks. The *Panzerjäger* or tank hunter sections of *Totenkopf*, although usually equipped with conventional anti-tank guns, often used tank destroyers. These provided the anti-tank sections with considerably more tactical flexibility and mobility.

When the Germans invaded the Soviet Union in 1941, they met the Soviet T-34 and KV-1 tanks, which were superior to the German armour and were largely impervious to the light anti-tank guns used by the *Wehrmacht* and *Waffen-SS*. Thus the Germans were forced to take a number of expedient measures to counter this new threat.

One such improvisation was the *Marder*, which mounted a 75mm Pak 40 on the chassis of a Pz Kpfw38(t). This measure proved reasonably successful, as did the *Marder* II, both which served with *Totenkopf*. The *Jadgpanzer* IV was a tank-hunter version of the PzKpfw IV. Its 75mm gun was housed in the superstructure of the chassis. This provided a low silhouette and the tank proved popular with *Panzerjäger* troops. In late 1944, the *Jadgpanzer* IV was modified to take a 70-calibre gun. These vehicles were effective and powerful tank-killers.

JADGPANZER IV
Crew: 4
Weight: 2580kg
Length: 8.58m
Width: 2.93m
Height: 1.69m
Armament: 1 x 75mm Pak 39 gun, 2 x 7.92mm machine guns
Powerplant: Maybach HL 120 12-cylinder engine – 265hp

Performance: Speed (road) – 25kmh; range (road) – 214km

MARDER III
Crew: 4
Weight: 1100kg
Length: 4.65m
Width: 2.35m
Height: 2.48m
Armament: 75mm Pak 40 gun, 1 x 7.92mm machine gun
Powerplant: Praga AC – 150hp
Performance: Speed (road) – 42kmh; range (road) – 140km

SELF-PROPELLED ARTILLERY

In Guderian's theory, the perfect panzer formation would contain its own artillery on self-propelled mounts, thus providing rapid and mobile fire support as and when required by the assaulting panzers. Unfortunately for the Germans, such equipment remained rare throughout the war; most of their artillery still had to be towed. Nonetheless, a number of self-propelled guns did provide very useful artillery support in some formations.

It was soon clear that the small PzKpfw II was obsolete, but, as it was in production and quite reliable, it was selected as a carrier for self-propelled artillery. A 105mm leFH 18 howitzer was mounted on the top of the chassis behind an open-topped armoured shield. The result was known as the *Wespe*, which *Totenkopf* began to receive for its new armoured artillery battalions in the winter of 1942–43. It proved a very successful self-propelled weapon with a reputation for reliability and mobility.

WESPE
Crew: 5
Weight: 11,000kg
Length: 4.81m
Width: 2.28m
Height: 2.3m
Armament: 105mm leFH 18 howitzer, 1 x 7.92mm machine gun

Above: A battery of *Hummel* self-propelled guns mounting 150mm sFH 18 howitzers. The *Hummel* was an excellent self-propelled gun, mixing mobility with firepower, but the division never had enough for its needs.

Powerplant: 1 Maybach 6-cylinder engine – 140hp
Performance: Speed (road) – 40kmh; range (road) – 220km

When it came to mounting a larger howitzer on a self-propelled chassis, the Germans were forced to put the gun on top of a PzKpfw III and IV tank hybrid. It used a lengthened PzKpfw IV suspension and running gear combined with the final drive assemblies and track and transmission of a PzKpfw III. It mounted a 150mm FH18 field howitzer. The resulting vehicle was called the *Hummel* and it formed the single mobile heavy

field artillery battery for *Totenkopf* from the spring of 1943. It proved a useful and popular weapon, and was probably the best example of German purpose-built self-propelled artillery. Here at last was an artillery piece that could fight at the pace of the panzers.

HUMMEL
Crew: 5
Weight: 24000kg
Length: 7.17m
Width: 2.87m
Height: 2.81m
Armament: 1 x 15cm sFH FH18 howitzer, 1 x 7.92mm machine gun
Powerplant: Maybach V12 engine – 265hp
Performance: Speed (road) – 42kmh; range (road) – 215km

TOTENKOPF'S WAR SERVICE

Date	Corps	Army	Army Group	Location
12.39	Reserve	OKH	-	Stuttgart
1.40 - 5.40	Reserve	OKH	-	Alzey/Brilon
6.40	Reserve	-	B	North France, Bordeaux
7.40 - 8.40	XIV	2nd Army	C	Bordeaux
9.40 - 10.40	-	7th Army	C	Bordeaux
11.40 - 12.40	XXXI	7th Army	D	Bordeaux
1.41 - 4.41	XXXIX	7th Army	D	Dax, Mont-de-Marsan
5.41	XXXI	7th Army	D	Dax, Mont-de-Marsan
6.41	-	4th Panzer Group	North	Kovno
7.41	LVI	4th Panzer Group	North	Pleskau
8.41	XXVIII	16th Army	North	Luga, Waldai
9.41	LVI	16th Army	North	Demyansk
10.41 - 2.42	X	16th Army	North	Demyansk
3.42 - 9.42	II	16th Army	North	Demyansk
10.42*	X	16th Army	North	Demyansk
11.42	Reserve	-	D	South France
12.42	Reserve	1st Army	D	Perpignan
1.43 - 2.43	Reserve	-	D	South France
3.43	SS Panzerkorps	4th Panzer Army	South	Kharkov
4.43	Raus	Kempf	South	Kharkov
5.43	Reserve	Kempf	South	Kharkov
6.43	replenishing	-	South	Kharkov
7.43	II. SS	4th Panzer Army	South	Belgorod
8.43	Reserve	6th Army	South	Stalino
9.43	XXXXVII	8th Army	South	Dniepr
10.43	XI	8th Army	South	Dniepr
11.43 - 12.43	LII	1st Pz. Army	South	Krivoi-Rog
1.44	LVII	6th Army	South	Krivoi-Rog
2.44	Schmidt	8th Army	South	Cherkassy
3.44	XXXX	8th Army	South	Cherkassy
4.44	VII	8th Army	South Ukraine	Kishinev
5.44	LXVII	8th Army	South Ukraine	Roman
6.44	Reserve	8th Army	South Ukraine	Roman
7.44	VI	4th Army	Centre	Bialystok
8.44 - 11.44	IV. SS	9th Army	Centre	Modlin
12.44	IV. SS	-	Centre	Modlin
1.45	Reserve	-	South	Hungary
2.45 - 3.45	IV. SS	6th Army	South	Hungary
4.45	II. SS	6th Army	South	Vienna
5.45	II. SS	6th Army	Ostmark	Linz

* part of the division had moved to South France 10.42 (Aufstellungsstab, LXXXIII. Corps/Army Group Felber). Source: Jason Pipes

WAFFEN-SS RANKS AND THEIR ENGLISH EQUIVALENTS

SS-Schütze	Private	SS-Hauptsturmführer	Captain
SS-Oberschütze	Senior Private, attained after six months' service	SS-Sturmbannführer	Major
		SS-Oberbannsturmführer	Lieutenant-Colonel
SS-Sturmmann	Lance-Corporal	SS-Standartenführer	Colonel
SS-Rottenführer	Corporal	SS-Oberführer	Senior Colonel
SS-Unterscharführer	Senior Corporal /Lance-Sergeant	SS-Brigadeführer und Generalmajor der Waffen-SS	Major-General
SS-Scharführer	Sergeant	SS-Gruppenführer und	Lieutenant-General
SS-Oberscharführer	Staff Sergeant	Generalleutnant der Waffen-SS	
SS-Hauptscharführer	Warrant Officer	SS-Obergruppenführer	General
SS-Sturmscharführer	Senior Warrant Officer after 15 years' service	und General der Waffen-SS	
		SS-Oberstgruppenführer	Colonel-General
SS-Untersturmführer	Second Lieutenant	und Generaloberst der Waffen-SS	
SS-Obersturmführer	First Lieutenant	Reichsführer-SS	(no English equivalent)

TOTENKOPF TANK INVENTORY – KURSK 1943

Date	III (L)	IV (S)	IV (L)	VI	Command	Subtotal	A/G	Total
1 July	63	8	44	15	9	139	35	174
4 July	59	5	42	11	8	125	28	153
8 July	52	7	28	5	7	99	13	112
9 July	47	7	20	2	5	81	12	93
10 July	48	7	21	2	5	83	21	104
11 July	54	4	26	10	7	101	20	121
13 July	32	3	14	-	5	54	20	74
15 July	28	3	17	7	6	61	20	81
16 July	30	4	23	9	7	73	20	93

III (L) – PzKpfw III long barrel
IV (S)- PzKpfw IV short barrel
IV (L) – PzKpfw IV long barrel
VI – PzKpfw VI Tiger
Command – Command tanks
A/G – Assault gun

Source: David M. Glantz and Jonathan M. House, *The Battle of Kursk*, Ian Allan, 1999.

TOTENKOPF COMMANDERS

1.11.39–7.7.41 *Obergruppenführer* **Theodor Eicke**
7.7.41–18.7.41 *Obergruppenführer* **Matthias Kleinheisterkamp**
18.7.41–19.9.41 *Obergruppenführer* **Georg Keppler**
19.9.41–26.2.43 *Obergruppenführer* **Theodor Eicke**

26.6.43–27.4.43 *Obergruppenführer* **Hermann Priess**
27.4.43–15.5.43 *Gruppenführer* **Heinz Lammerding**
15.5.43–22.10.43 *Gruppenführer* **Max Simon**
22.10.43–21.6.44 *Obergruppenführer* **Hermann Priess**
21.6.44–8.5.45 *Brigadeführer* **Hellmuth Becker**

SELECT BIBLIOGRAPHY

Anyone interested in a more in-depth academic study of the *Totenkopf* Division should turn to this superlative divisional history:

Charles Sydnor, *Soldiers of Destruction: The SS Death's Head Division, 1933–1945*, Princetown University Press, 1977, revised 1990.

Other work on the division

Karl Ullrich, *Wie ein fels im Meer: 3 SS Panzerdivision Totenkopf in Bild* (3 vols), Munin Verlag, 1984-6.

There are large number of useful general works on the SS:

Christopher Ailsby, *SS: Roll of Infamy*, Brown Books, 1997.

Roger Bender and Hugh Taylor, *Uniforms, Organisation and History of the Waffen SS*, Vols 1-5, Bender, 1969-83.

Rupert Butler, *The Black Angels*, Sheridan, 1978.

Stephen Hart and Russell Hart, *Weapons and Fighting Tactics of the Waffen SS*, Spellmount, 1999.

Max Hastings, *Das Reich*, Michael Joseph, 1981.

Heinz Höhne, *The Order of the Death's Head*, Ballantine, 1967.

John Keegan, *Waffen-SS: The Asphalt Soldiers*, Ballantine, 1970.

Robert Lewis Koehl, *The Black Corps*, University of Wisconsin Press, 1983.

Robin Lumsden, *Himmler's Black Order, 1923-45*, Bramley, 1997.

Bruce Quarrie, *Weapons of the Waffen-SS*, PSL, 1988.

Gerald Reitlinger, *The SS: Alibi of a Nation, 1922-45*, the Viking Press, 1957.

George H. Stein, *The Waffen SS: Hitler's Elite Guard at War, 1939-45*, Cornell University Press, 1966.

Bernd Wegner, *The Waffen-SS: Organisation, Ideology and Function*, Blackwell, 1982.

Gordon Willamson, *Loyalty is My Honour*, Spellmount, 1997.

Gordon Willamson, *The SS: Hitler's Instrument of Terror*, Sidgwick and Jackson, 1994.

Gordon Willamson, *SS: The Blood Soaked Soil*, Blitz, 1997.

Martin Windrow, *The Waffen-SS*, Osprey, 1982.

There are a number of works relating to the La Paradis Masacre and it worth consulting the WO 309 series at the Public Record Office at Kew, London and the records at the Royal Norfolk Regiment, Norwich. See also:

Peter Hart, *At the Sharp End: From Le Paradis to Kohima*, Leo Cooper, 1998.

Cyril Jolly, *The Vengeance of Private Pooley*, Heinemann, 1958.

Cyril Jolly, *The Man Who Missed the Massacre*, Jolly, 1986.

P.K. Kemp, *History of the Royal Norfolk Regiment, 1919-51*, Vol 3, Regimental Association of the Royal Norfolk Regiment, 1953.

General works on Nazi Germany, the *Wehrmacht*, various campaigns and battles:

— *Battles Hitler Lost*, Richardson and Steirman, 1986.

Ian Bishop, *WWII: The Directory of Weapons*, Greenwich, 1998.

Paul Carrel, *Hitler Moves East, 1941-43*, Schiffer, 1965.

Paul Carrel, *Scorched Earth: Hitler's War on Russia 1943-44*, Schiffer, 1970.

Alan Clark, *Barbarossa*, Cassell, 1965.

Matthew Cooper and James Lucas, *Panzer*, Macdonald and Jane's, 1976.

Matthew Cooper and James Lucas, *Panzer Grenadiers*, Macdonald and Jane's, 1977.

I.C.B. Dear and M.R.D. Foot, *The Oxford Companion to the Second World War*, Oxford University Press, 1995.

Len Deighton, *Blitzkreig*, Grafton, 1981.

L.F. Ellis, *The War in France and Flanders*, HMSO, 1953.

John Erikson, *The Road to Stalingrad*, Weidenfeld and Nicolson, 1975.

John Erikson, *The Road to Berlin*, Weidenfeld and Nicolson, 1983.

Joachim Fest, *The Face of the Third Reich*, Penguin, 1963.

David M. Glantz and Jonathan M. House, *The Battle of Kursk*, Ian Allan, 1999.

Heinz Guderian, *Panzer Leader*, Futura, 1952.

Mark Healy, *Kursk 1943*, Osprey, 1993.

Rudolf Höss, *Commandant of Auschwitz*, Weidenfeld and Nicolson, 1951.

Alistair Horne, *To Lose a Battle*, Papermac, 1969.

Matthew Hughes and Christopher Mann, *Inside Hitler's Germany*, Brassey's, 2000.

Roger Edwards, *Panzer: A Revolution in Warfare*, Arms and Armour, 1988.

Thomas Jentz, *Germany's Panther Tank*, Schiffer, 1995.

B.H. Liddel Hart, *History of the Second World War*, Perigee, 1970.

B.H. Liddel Hart, *The Other Side of the Hill*, Pan, 1948.

James Lucas, *War on the Eastern Front*, Greenhill, 1998.

Kenneth Macksey, *Panzer Division, The Mailed Fist*, Purnell, 1968.

Kenneth Macksey, *Rommel: Battles and Campaigns*, Arms and Armour, 1979.

Samuel Mitcham, *Hitler's Legions*, Leo Cooper, 1985.

Steven Newton, *German Battle Tactics on the Russian Front, 1941-45*, Schiffer, 1994.

Richard Overy, *Russia's War*, Allen Lane, 1997.

Bryan Perret, *Iron Fist*, Arms and Armour, 1995.

Bryan Perret, *Knights of the Black Cross*, Robert Hale, 1986.

Harrison Salisbury, *The 900 Days: The Seige of Leningrad*, Pan, 1969.

William Shirer, *The Rise and Fall of the Third Reich*, Simon and Schuster, 1960.

Harold Shukman (ed), *Stalin's Generals*, Weidenfeld and Nicolson, 1993.

Louis Snyder, *Encyclopedia of the Third Reich*, Wordsworth, 1976.

John Toland, *Hitler*, Wordsworth, 1976.